AF394675

Silent Land Åsa Sjöström

Bokförlaget Max Ström

At the edge of the field Beniamin stops, takes a sunflower with one hand and looks at me. I take his picture and he disappears again into the field of sunflowers, returning to a game of hide-and-seek with his younger brothers and sisters. The Gradinari family are proud of these sunflowers and the rich Moldovan soil that has made them explode with colour at the end of July.

For the past four years, I have visited the Gradinaris in the little hamlet of Chetrosu in the north of Moldova, one of Europe's poorest countries. The bumpy unpaved road that leads to their house starts at a recently renovated church. Every time I drive up the road towards their house, the youngest children, Beniamin, Iosif, Maria and Katrina, rush out to greet me. They jump in the car, hug me and hold my hands for the short stretch remaining to their home, where their mother, Zina, and occasionally their father, Ion, are waiting. The Gradinari family has nine children and grandchildren and seems to grow further each year, necessitating extensions to the house when money is available. The two oldest children have their own houses in the village, although they are often abroad to earn money, so Zina takes care of the grandchildren.

Life for the Gradinaris is like that of many families in Moldova: hard-working and essentially self-sufficient people who are often dependent on money sent home from overseas. In the summer, they eat fresh fruit and vegetables, and in the winter their diet is usually made up of broth and white, often stale, bread. The Gradinari house is unpainted and the façade is grey concrete. Inside, the walls are covered in brightly coloured and flowery wallpaper. On their small farm, they have the season's harvest and a catch of nutria furs, as well as a basic tractor, four guard dogs, cows, sheep, hens and ducks. Chained dogs guard every coop, and the latest crop. In winter, an old-fashioned stove built inside the wall between two rooms is fired up and remains in constant use to heat just these rooms, where the family now lives for the season, while the rest of the house is left cold. It is not uncommon for these fires to get out of control, and for walls or the roof to catch fire. The last time there was such a fire at the Gradinaris' house nobody was hurt, but the roof needed to be repaired. The repair was expensive and left the family with no money to sow their watermelon field. Ion went to France hoping to find work to support his family. He was unable to find a job that time, but managed to scrape together 100 euros to return home.

The image I took of Beniamin holding the sunflower that year became burned into my memory. The Gradinari family had moved me in a way that is hard to explain – over the years we had developed a symbiotic relationship as we have shared experiences and learned about each other. While I sometimes feel I gained more out of this connection, they were always eager for me to return. And I did, again and again.

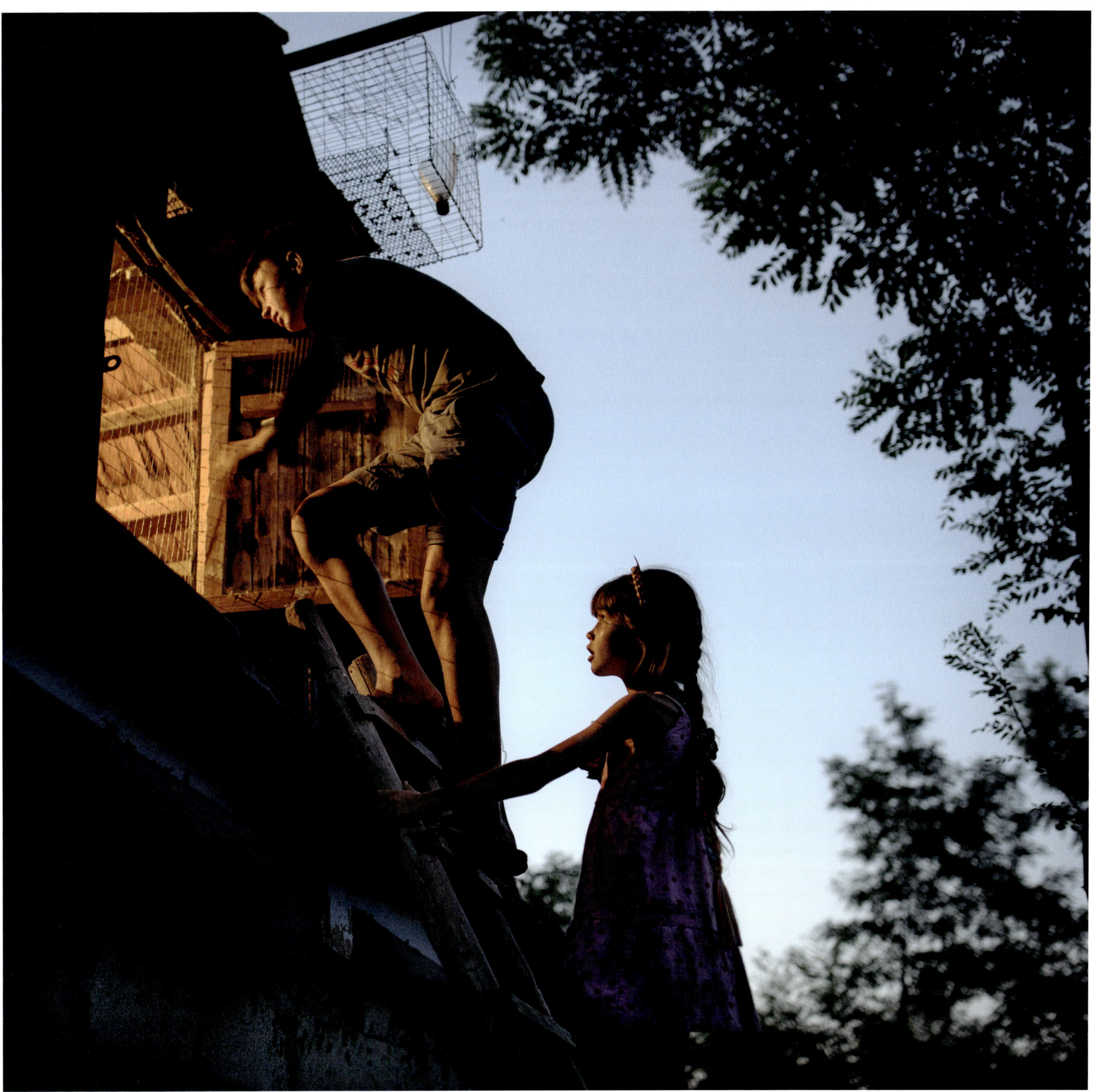

Iosif and Kristina Chetrosu 2017

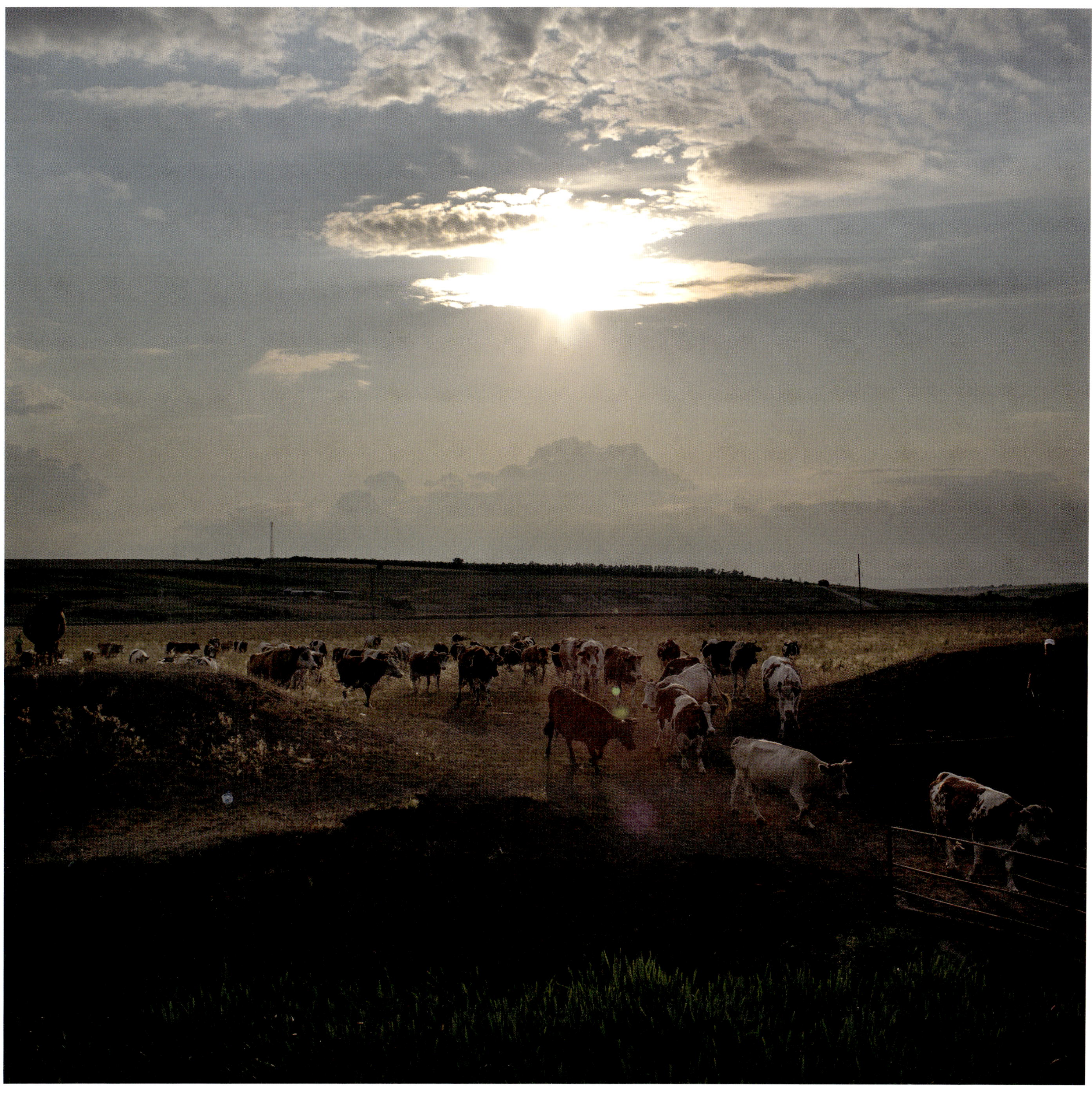

Chetrosu 2015

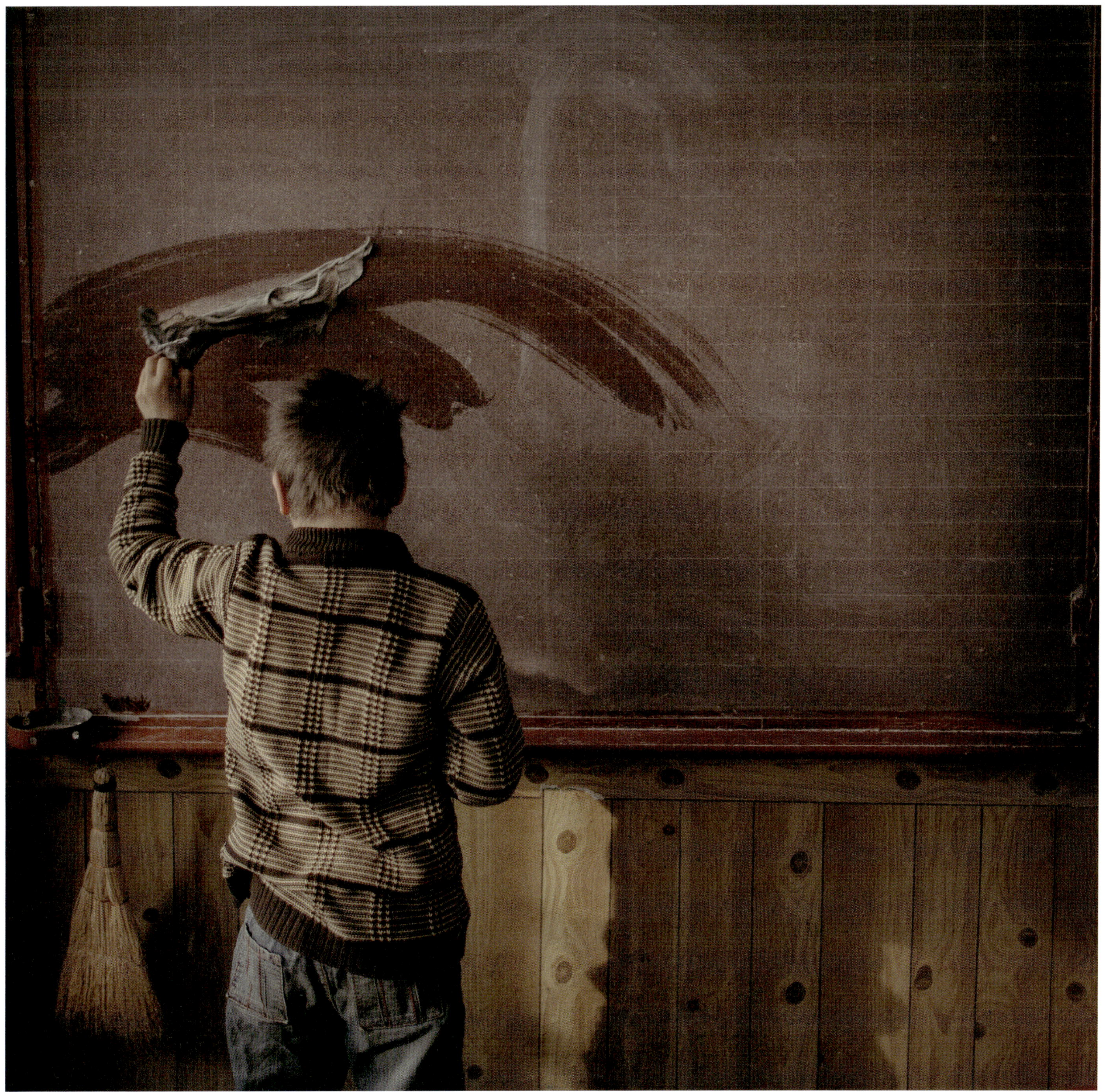

Igor, Baroncea 2014

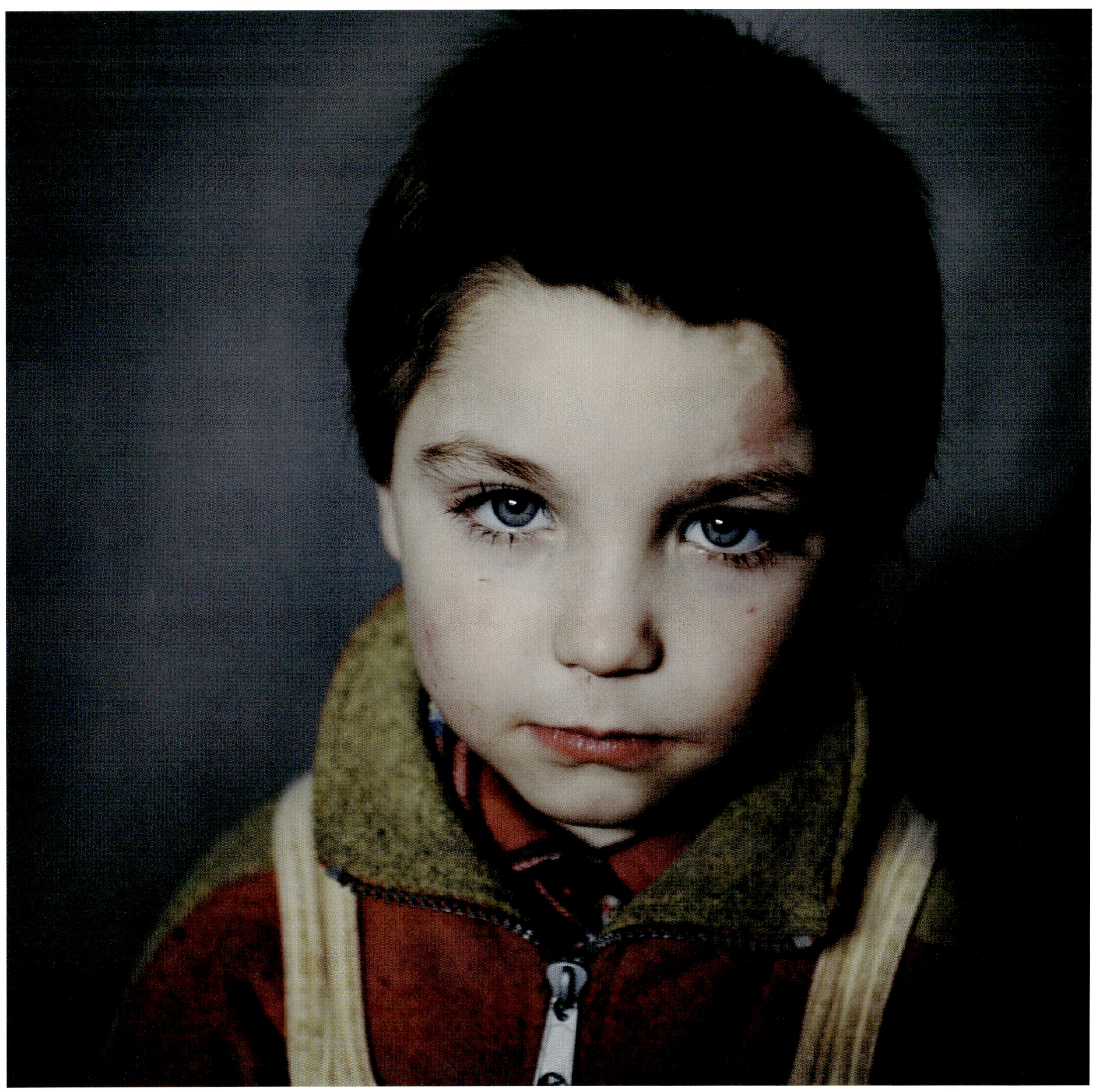

Son of an unknown father, Hîncești 2006

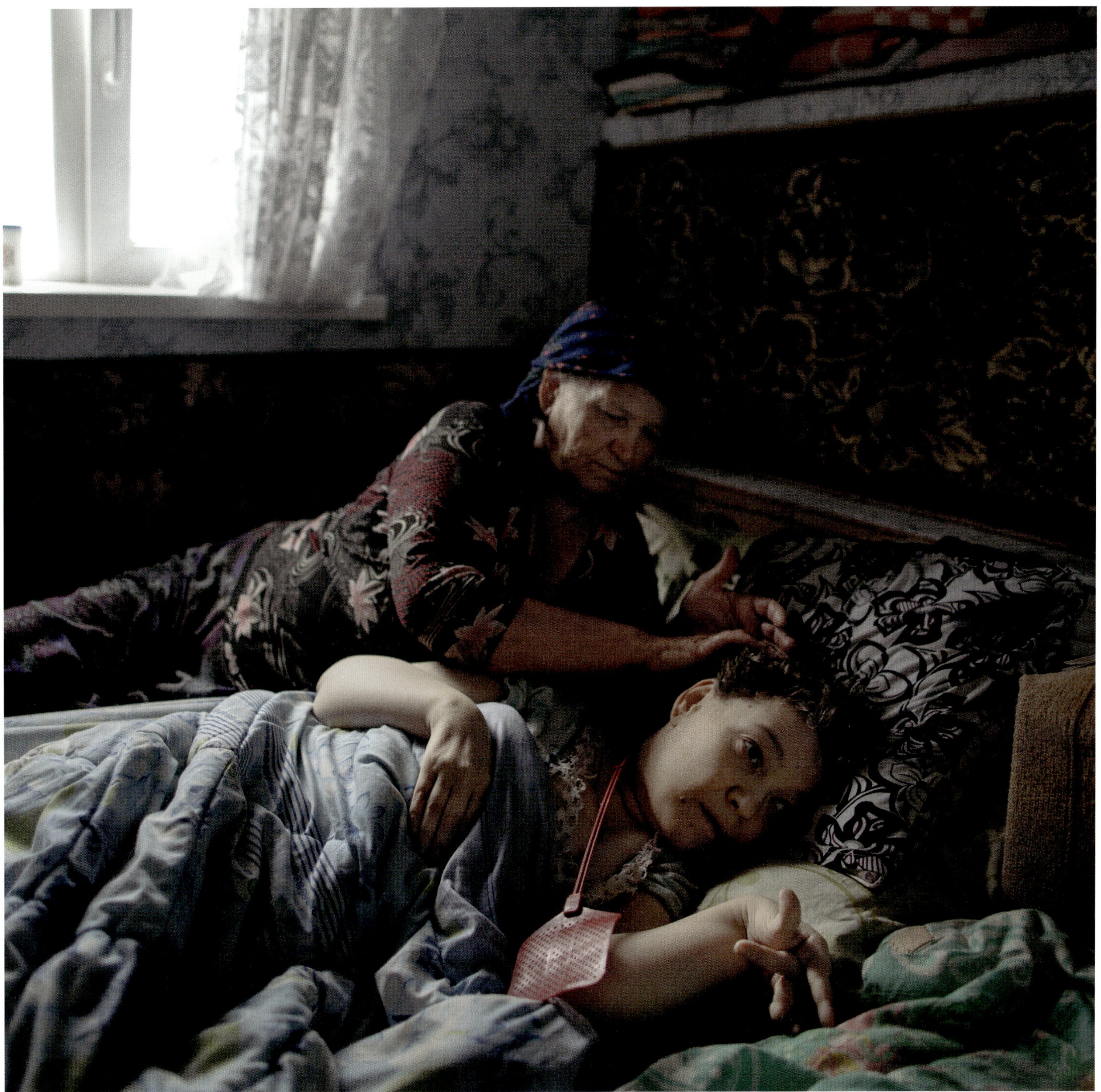

Olimpiada and her daughter Maria, Chetrosu 2016

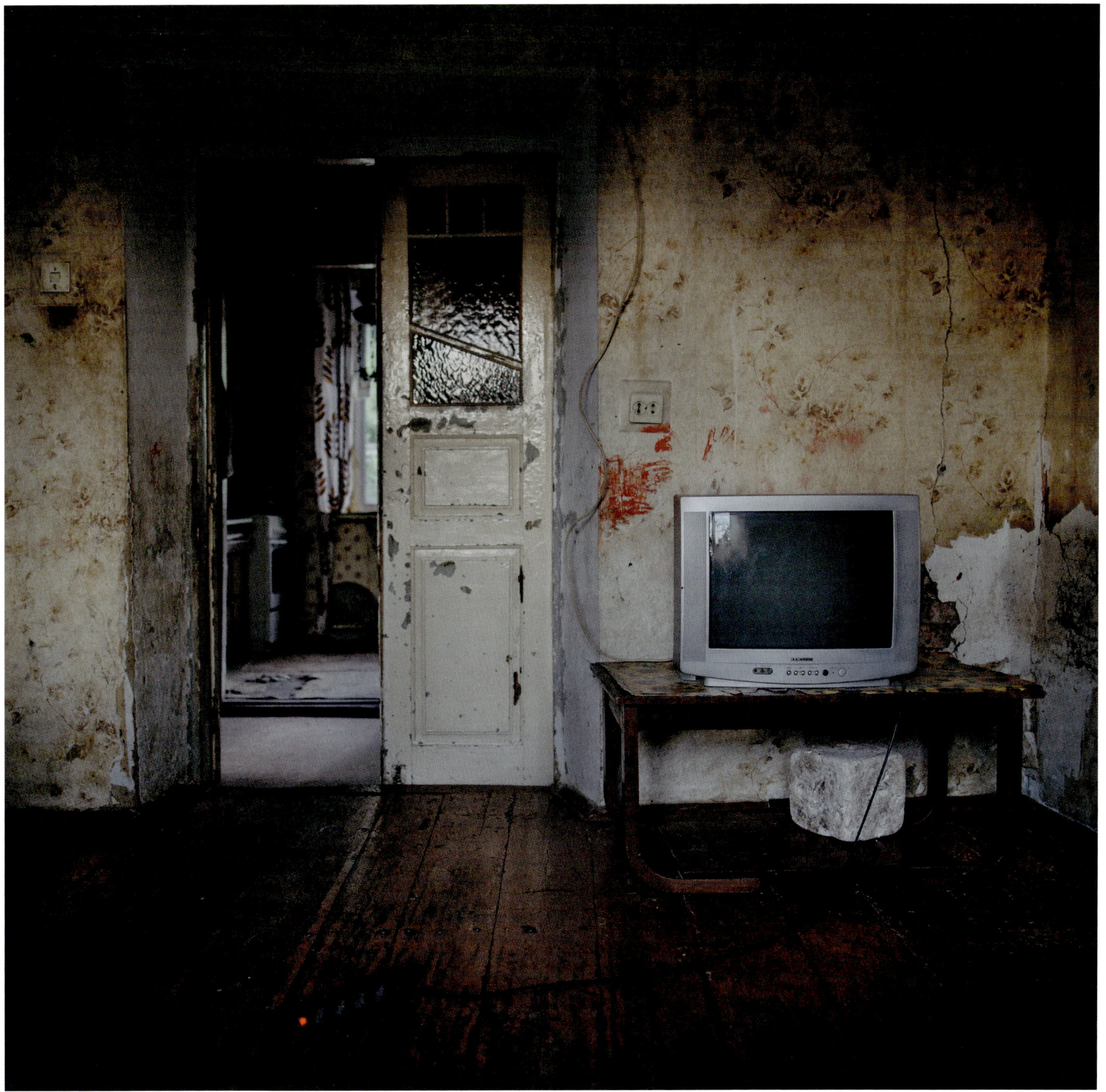

Codru 2015

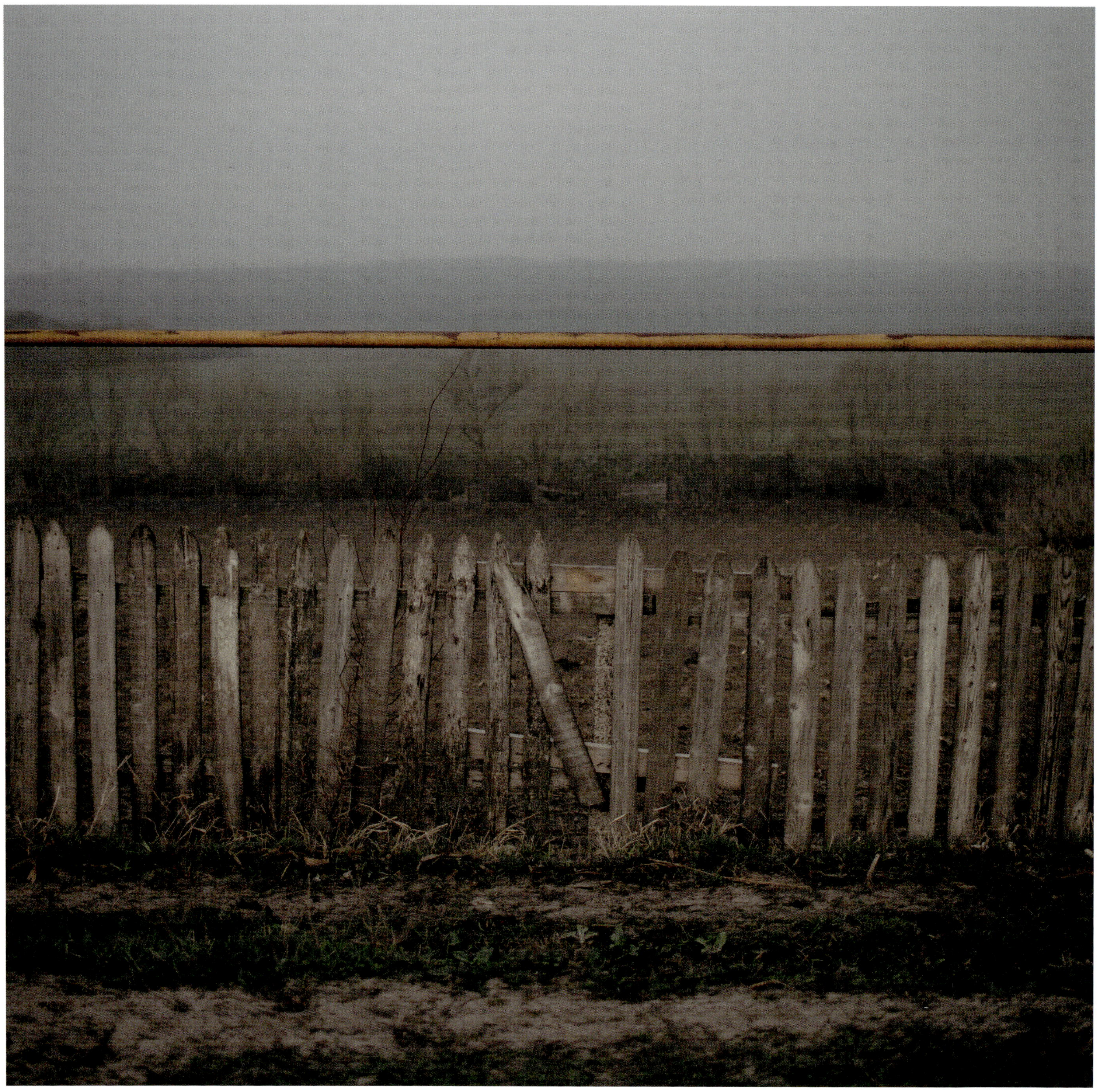

Baroncea 2014

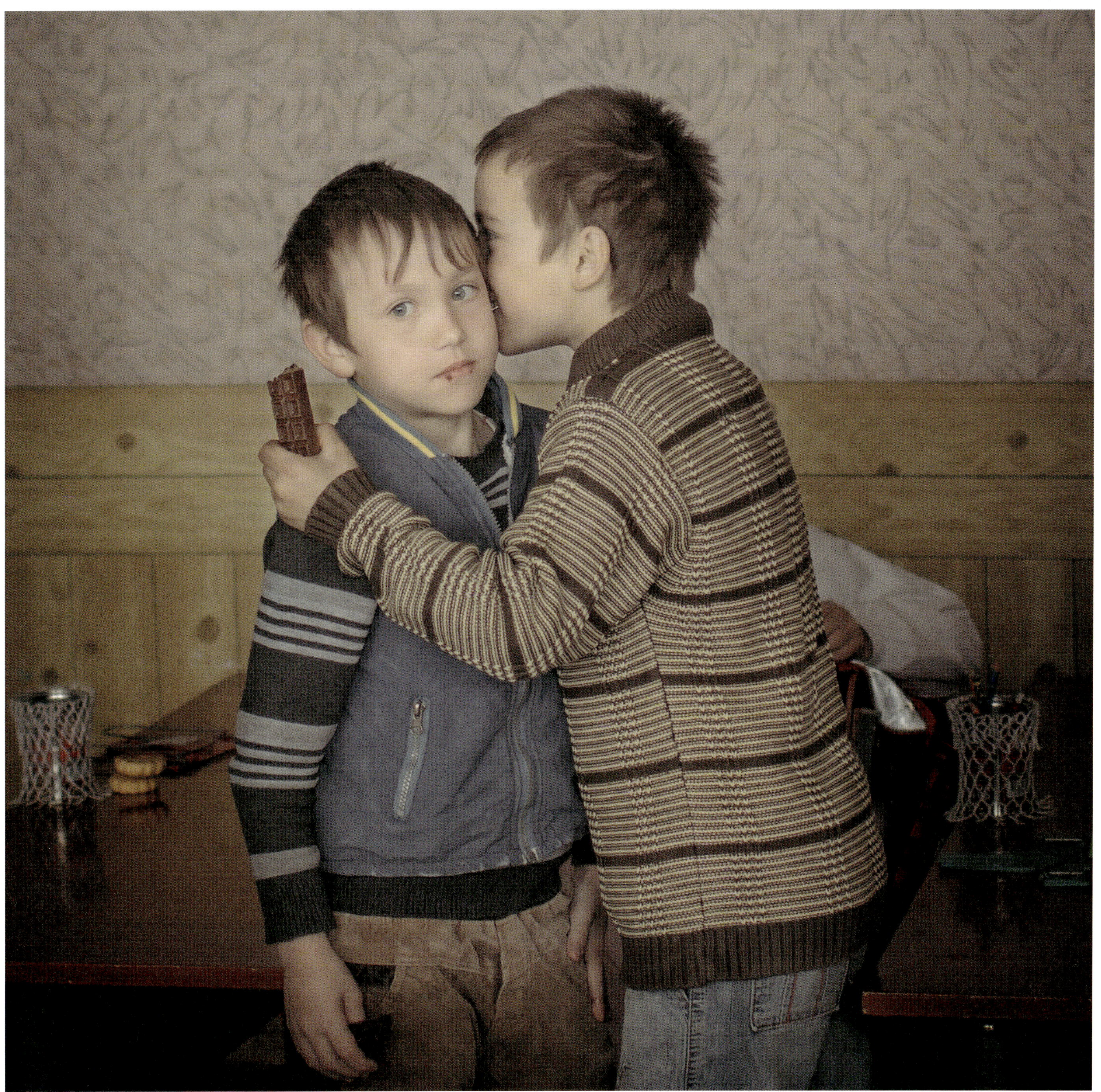

Birthday boys, Baroncea 2014

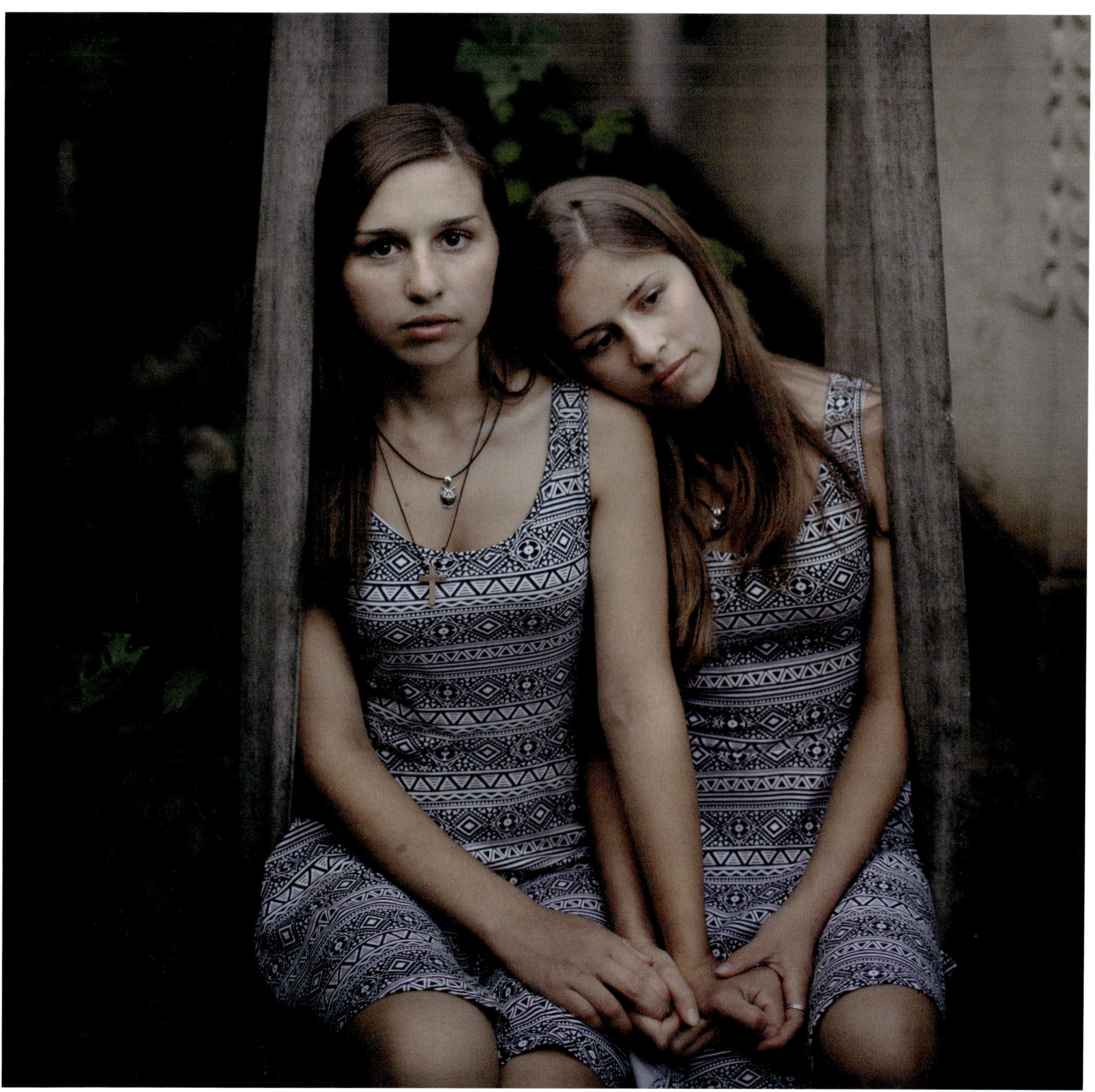

Karina and Mihaela Dumitraschuk, Doroțcaia 2015

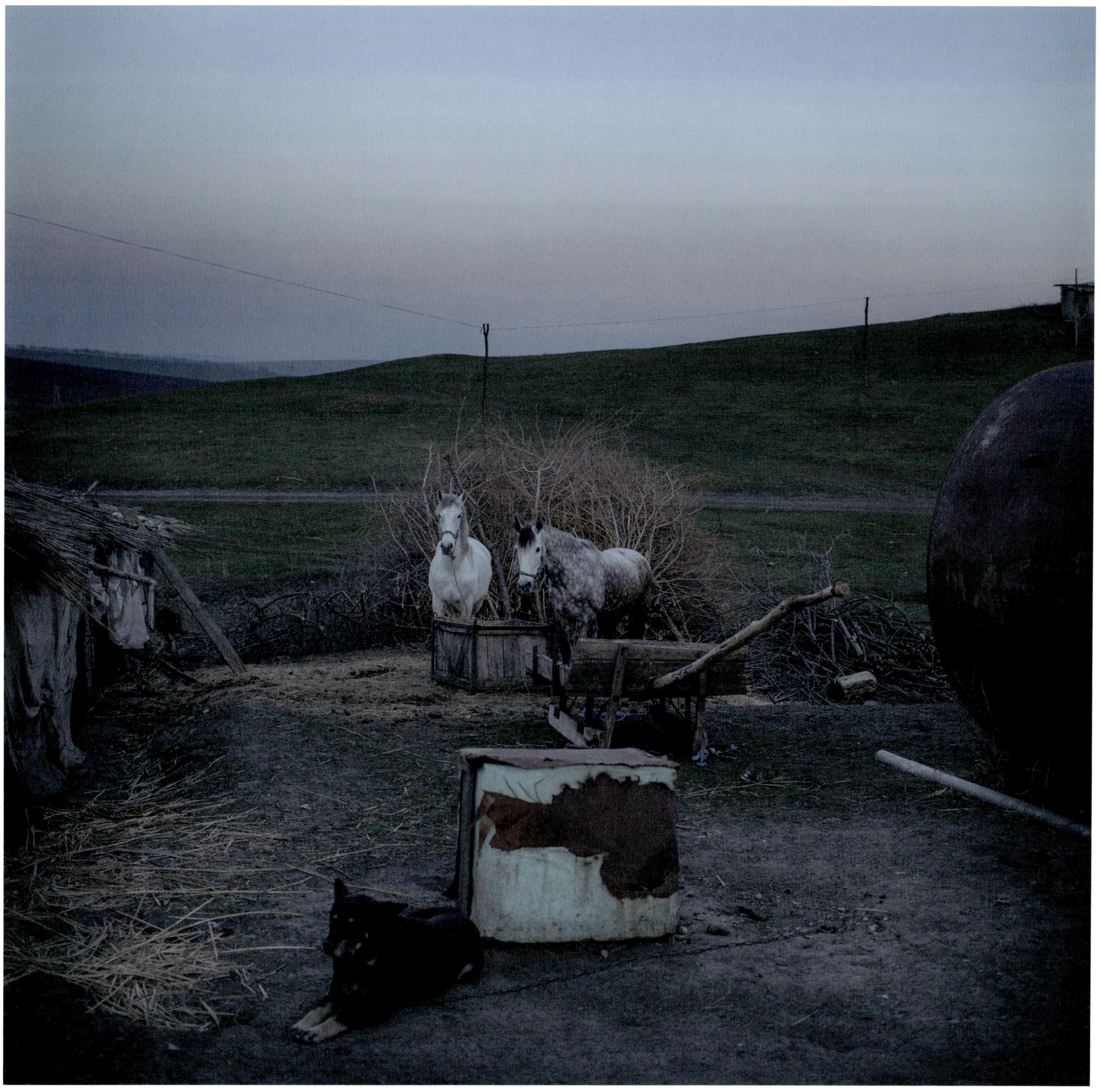

Moldova 2014

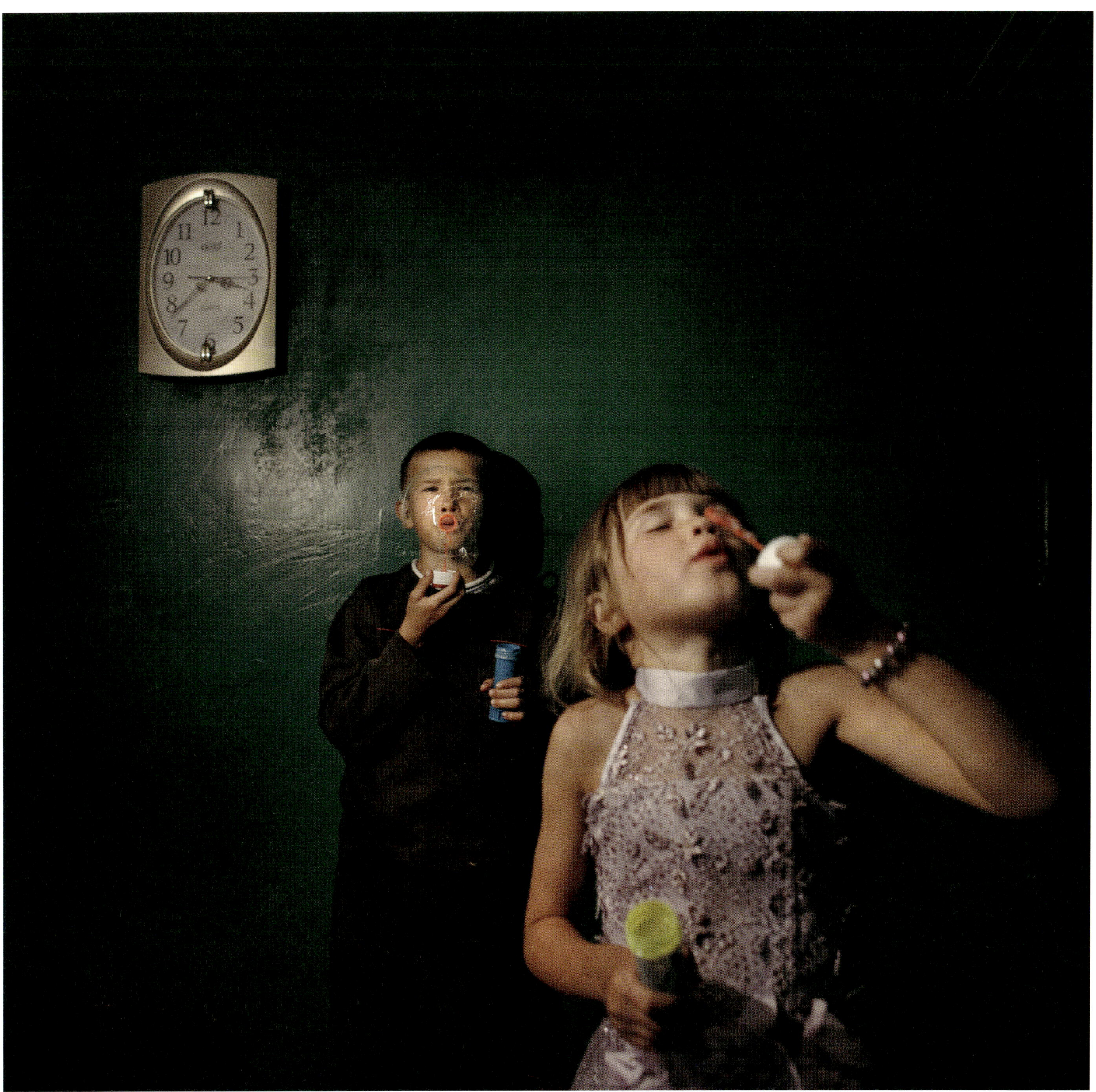

Beniamin and Karina, Chetrosu 2015

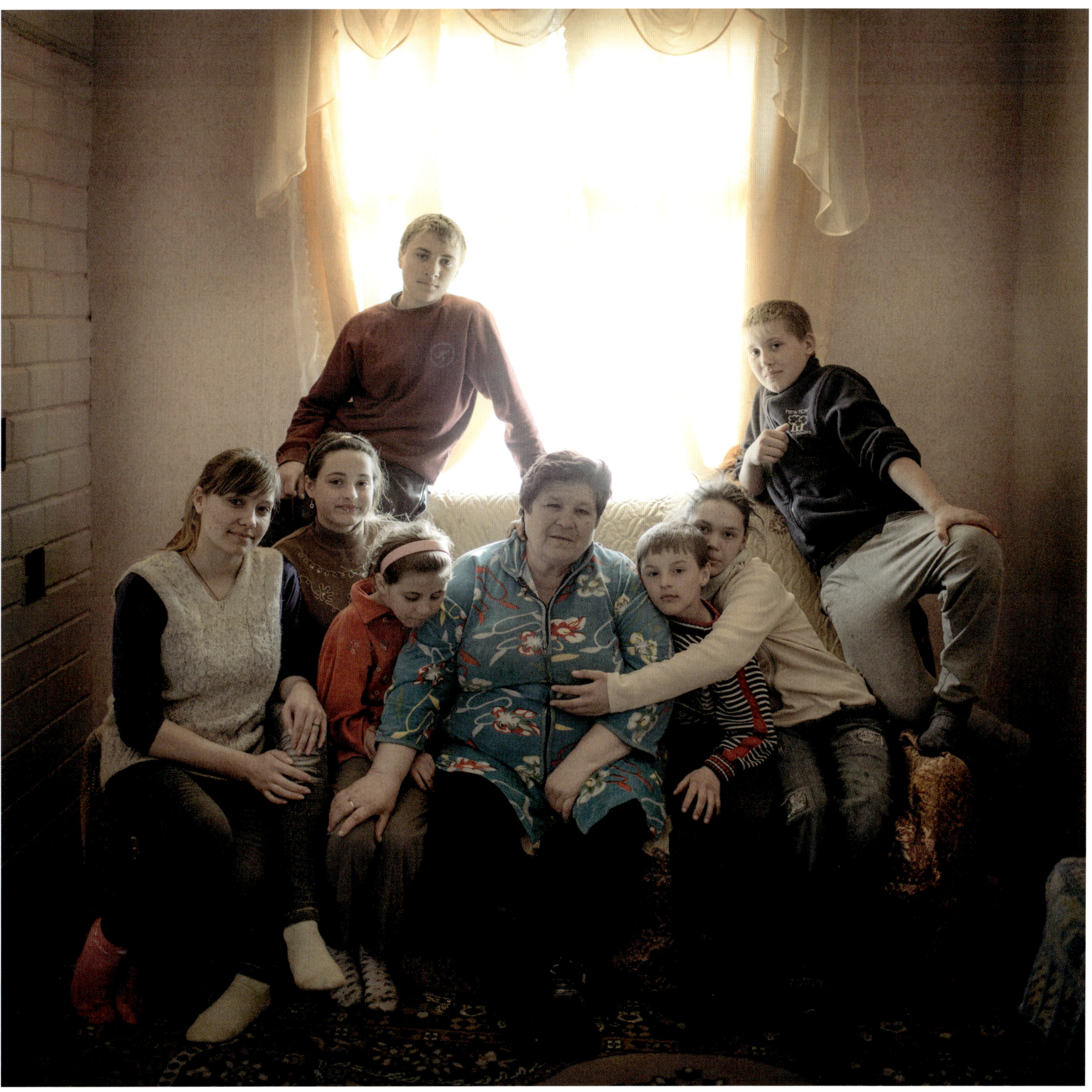

Garlia and her orphan children, Moara de Piatră 2014

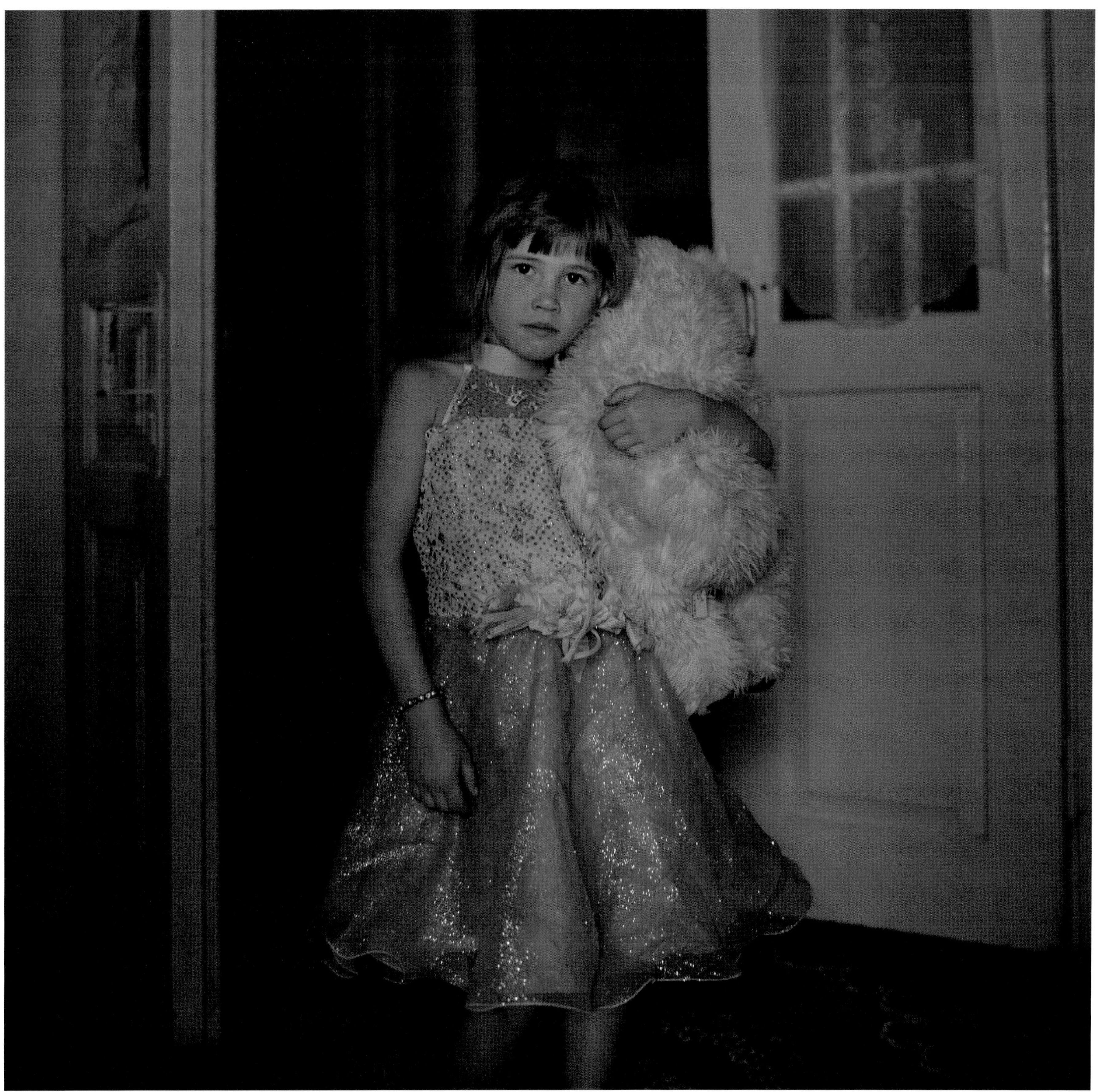

Kristina, Chetrosu 2015

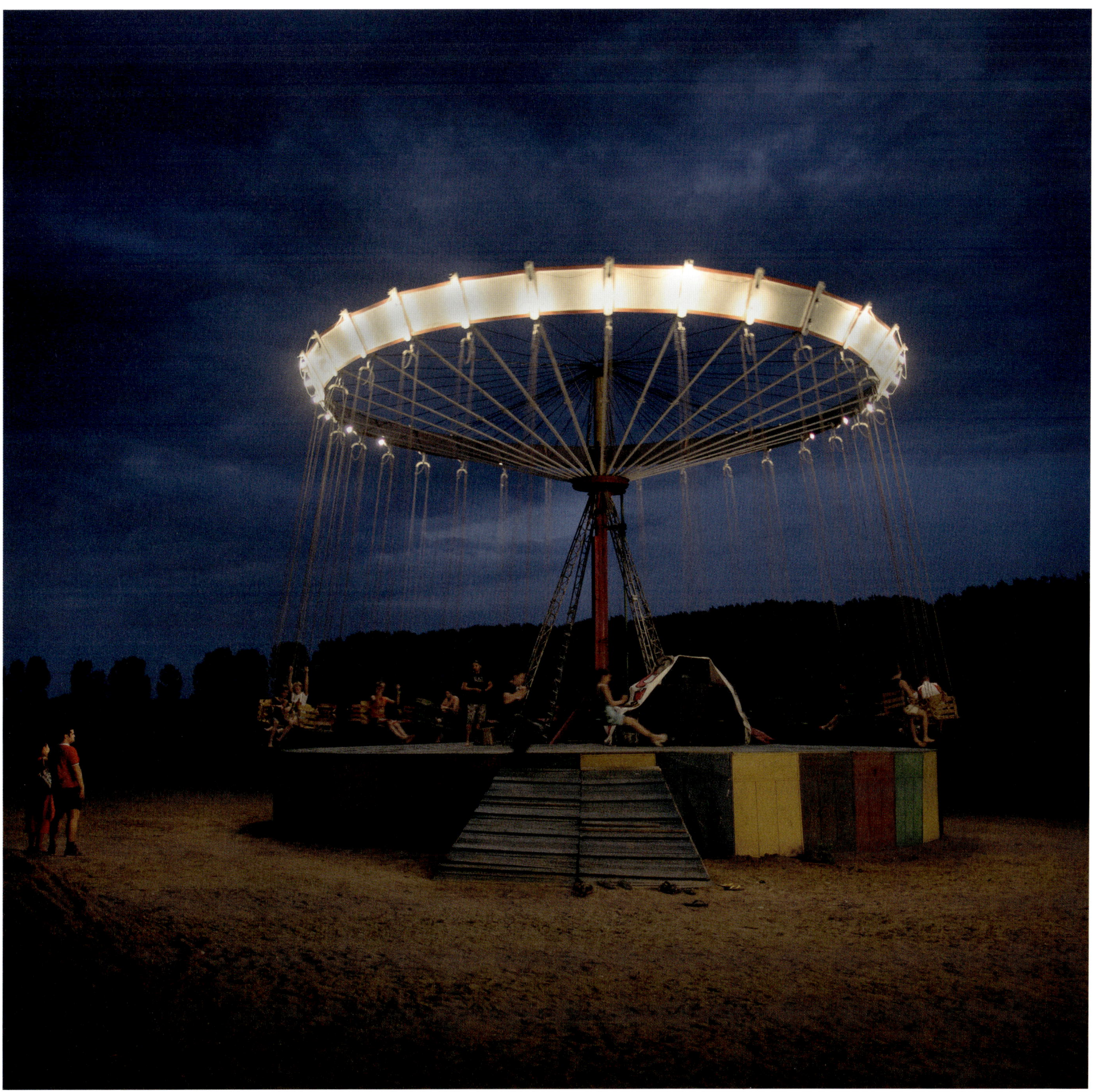

Vadul lui Vodă 2015

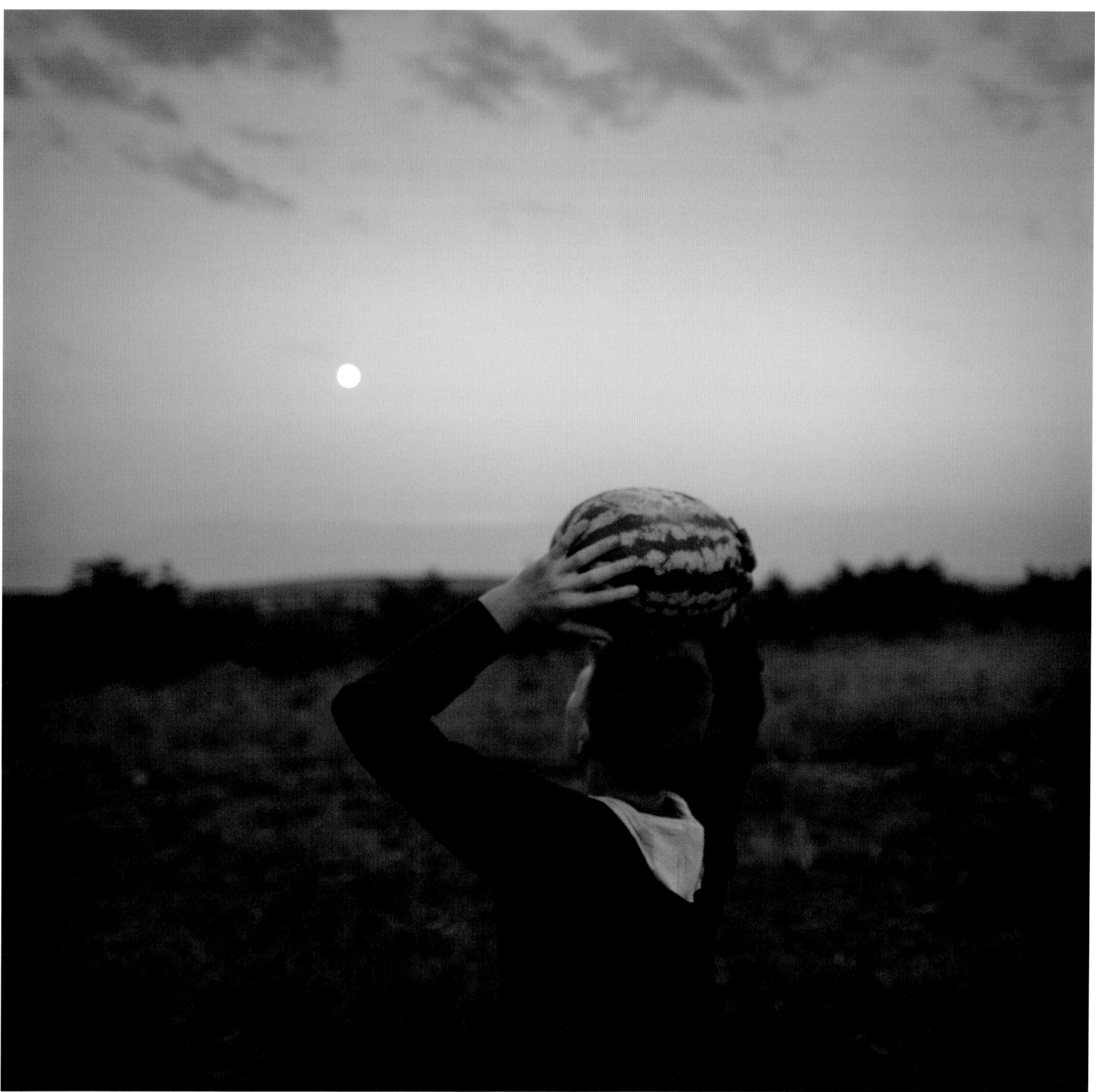

Iosif, Chetrosu 2016

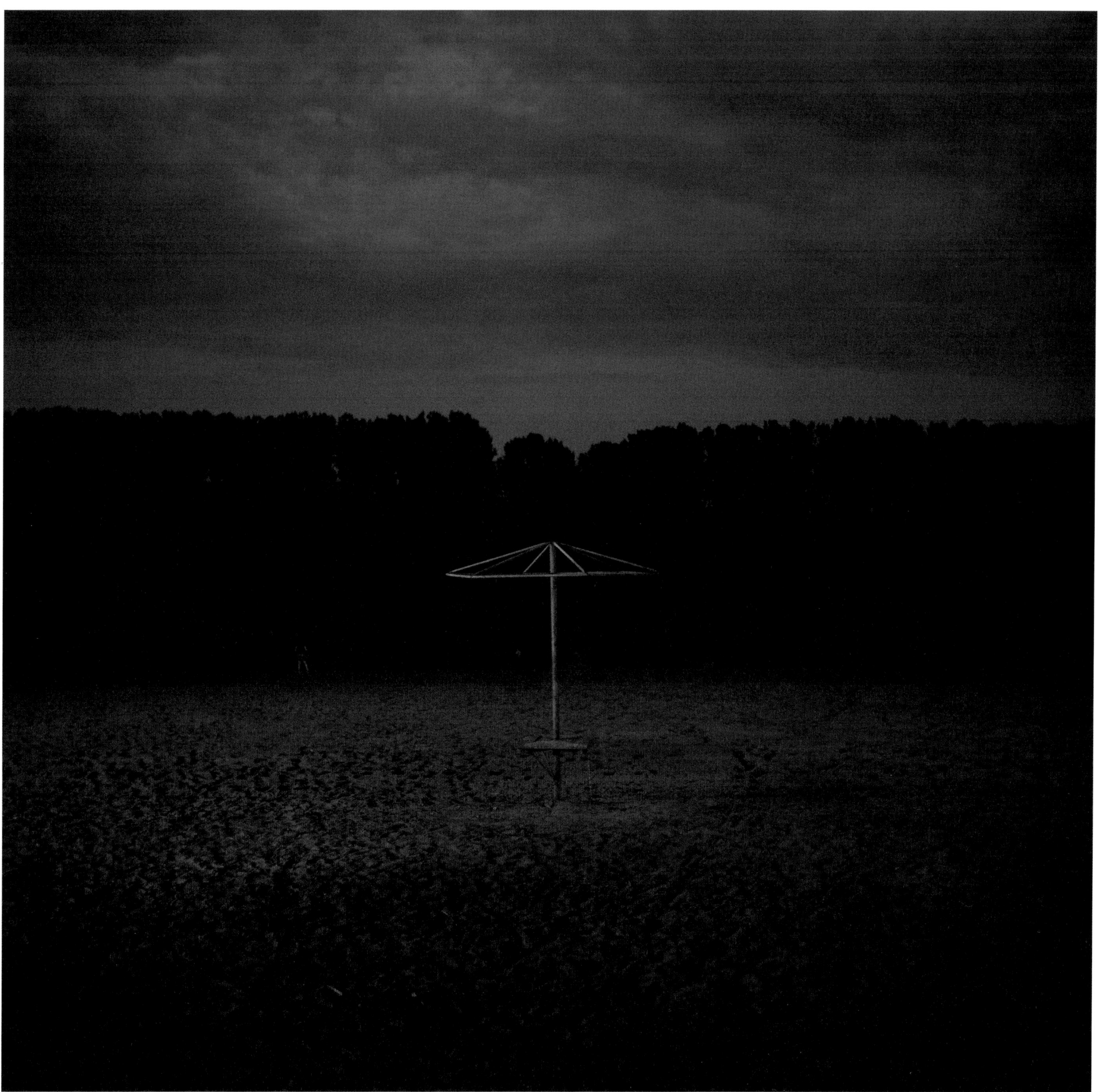

Vadul lui Vodă 2015

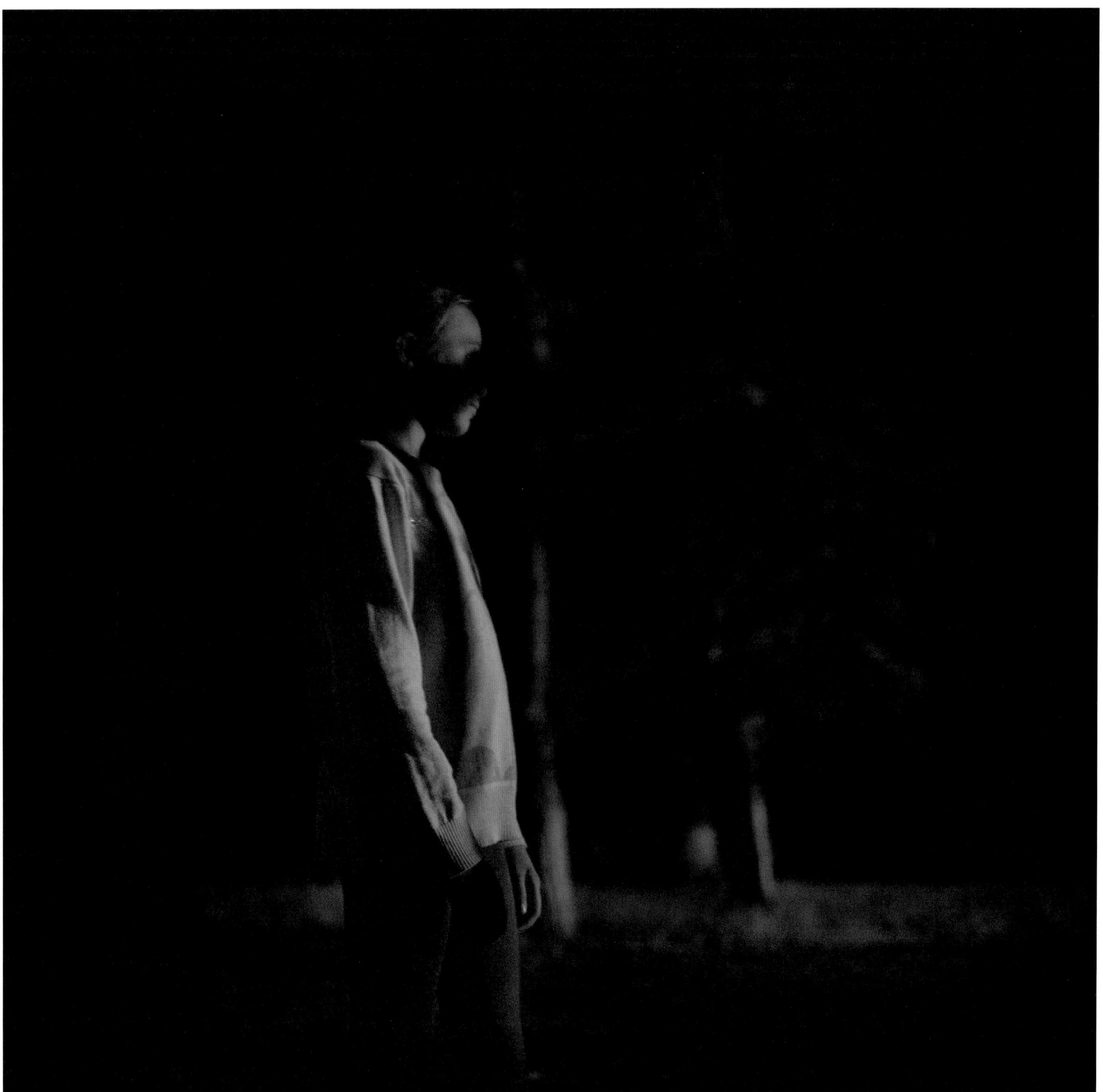

Maria, Chetrosu 2016

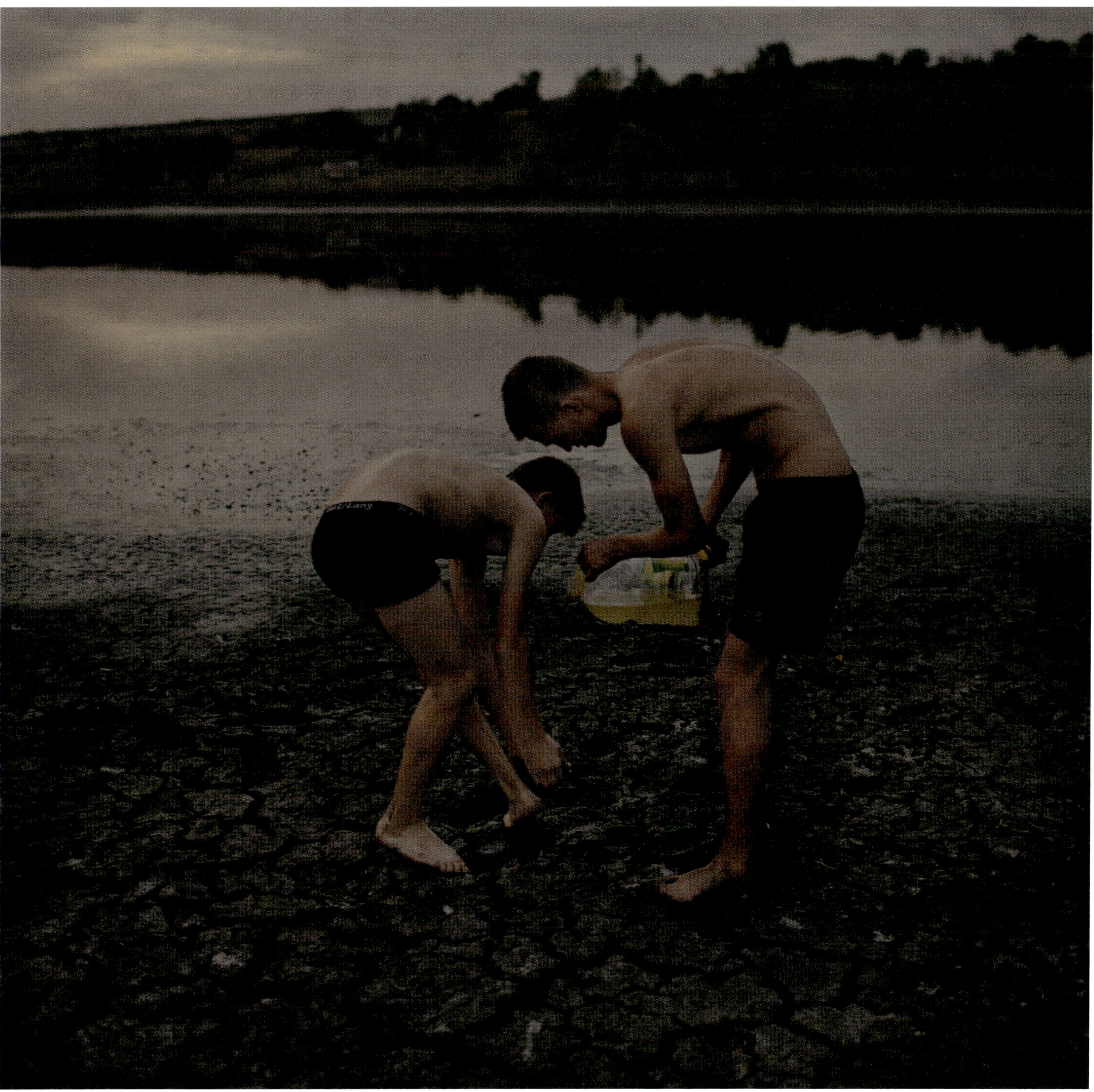

Iosif and Mihail, Chetrosu 2016

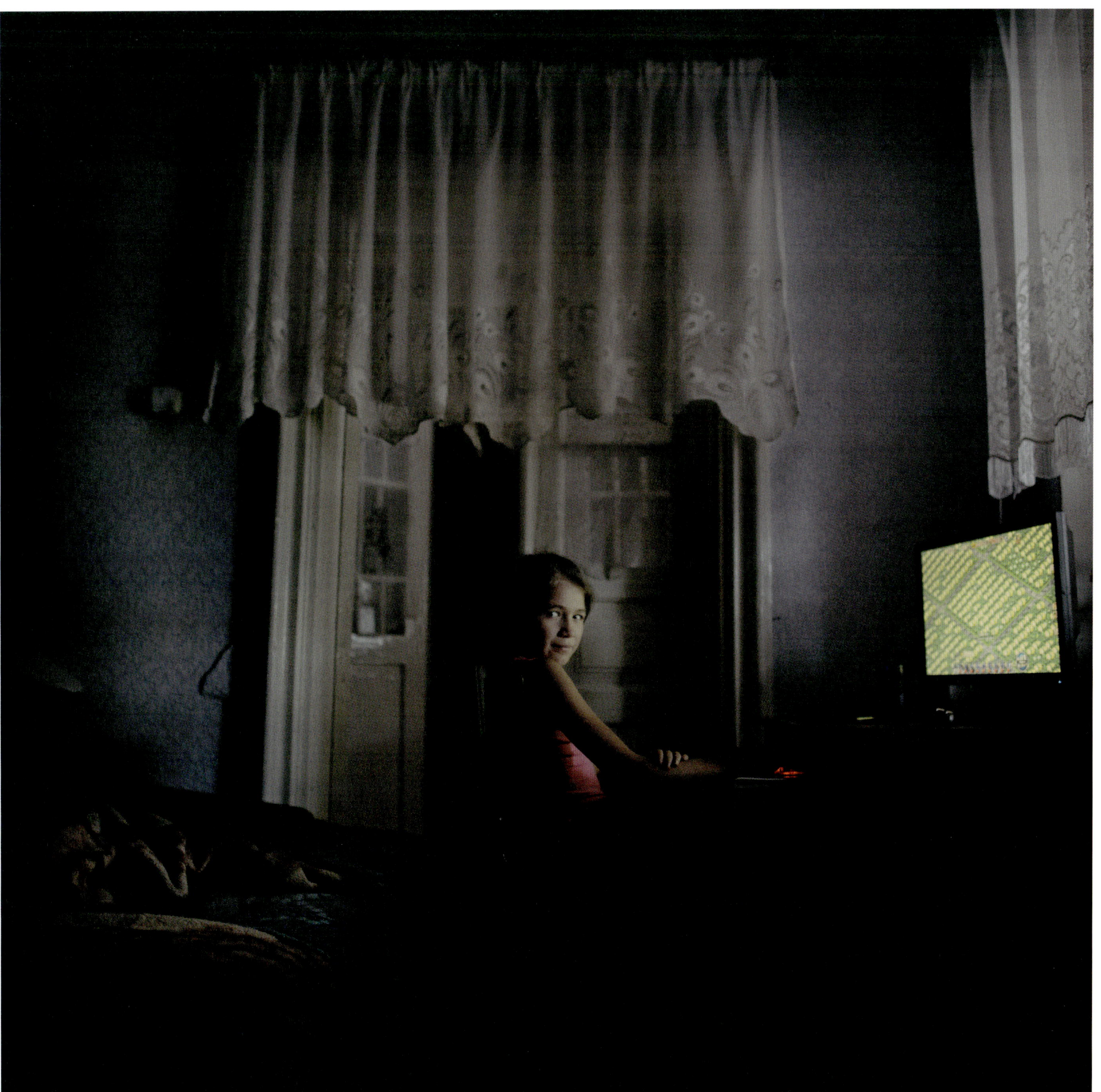

Maria, Chetrosu 2015

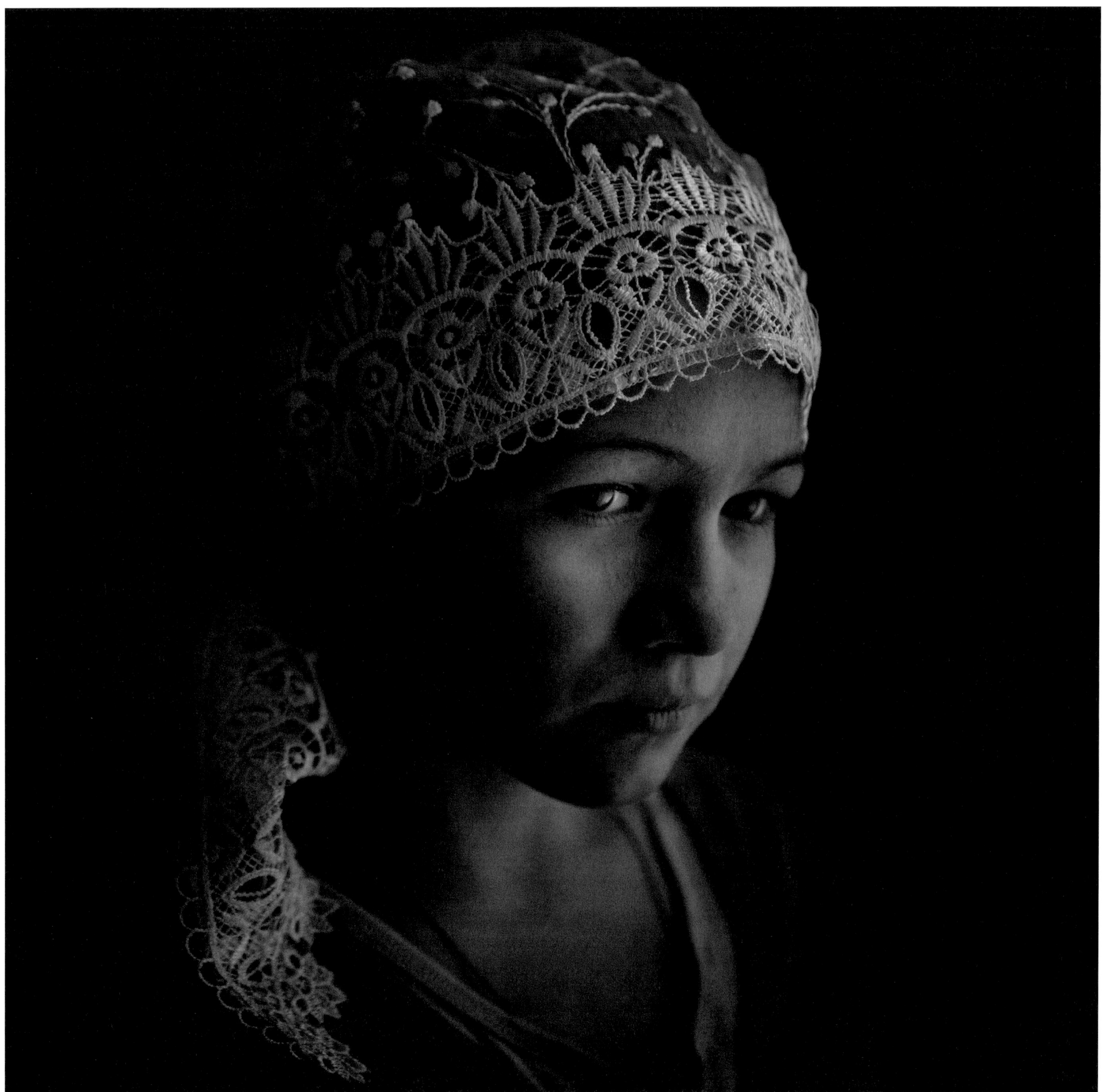

Maria, Chetrosu 2017

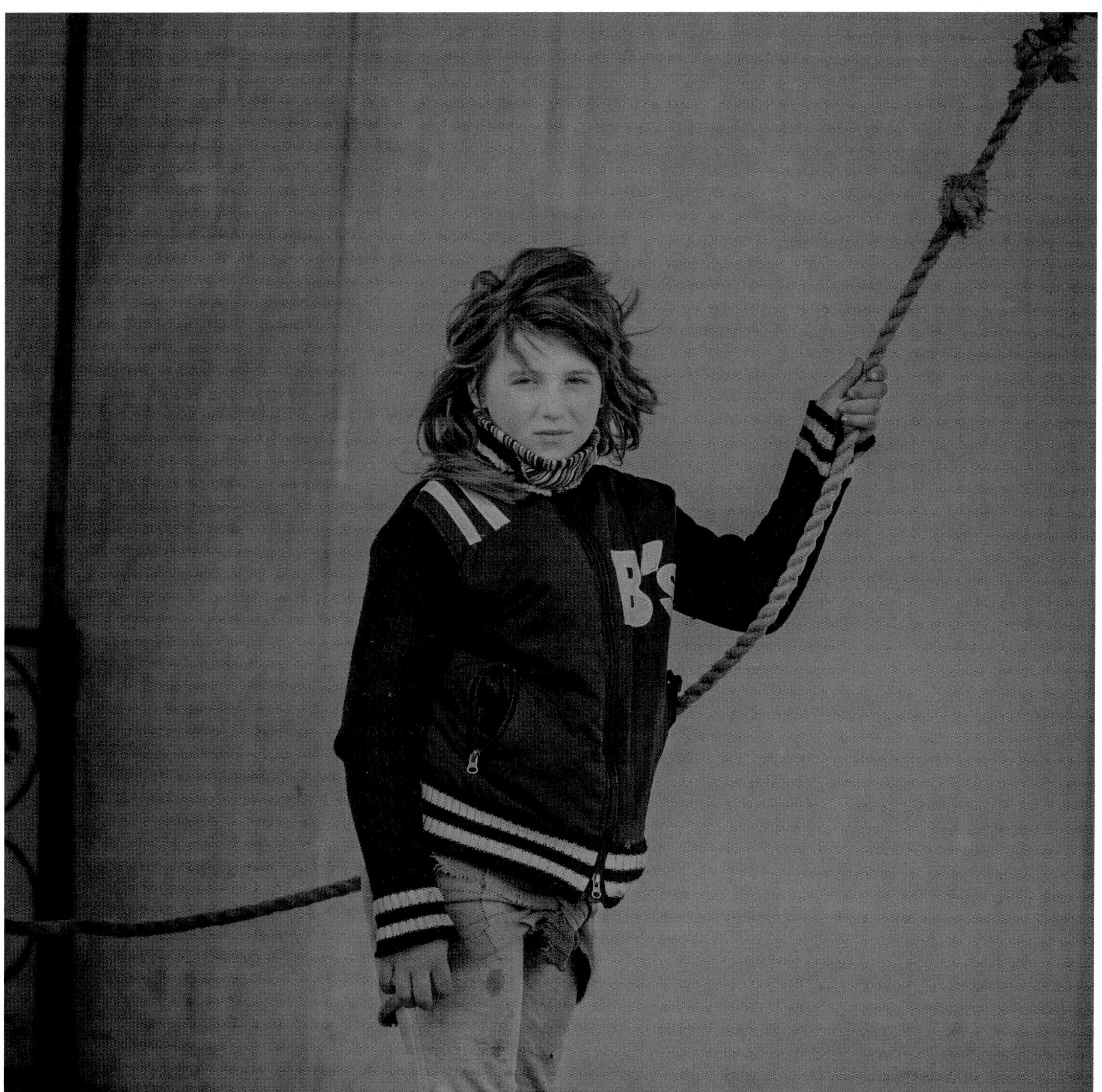

Antonia, Chiţcani Transnistria 2014

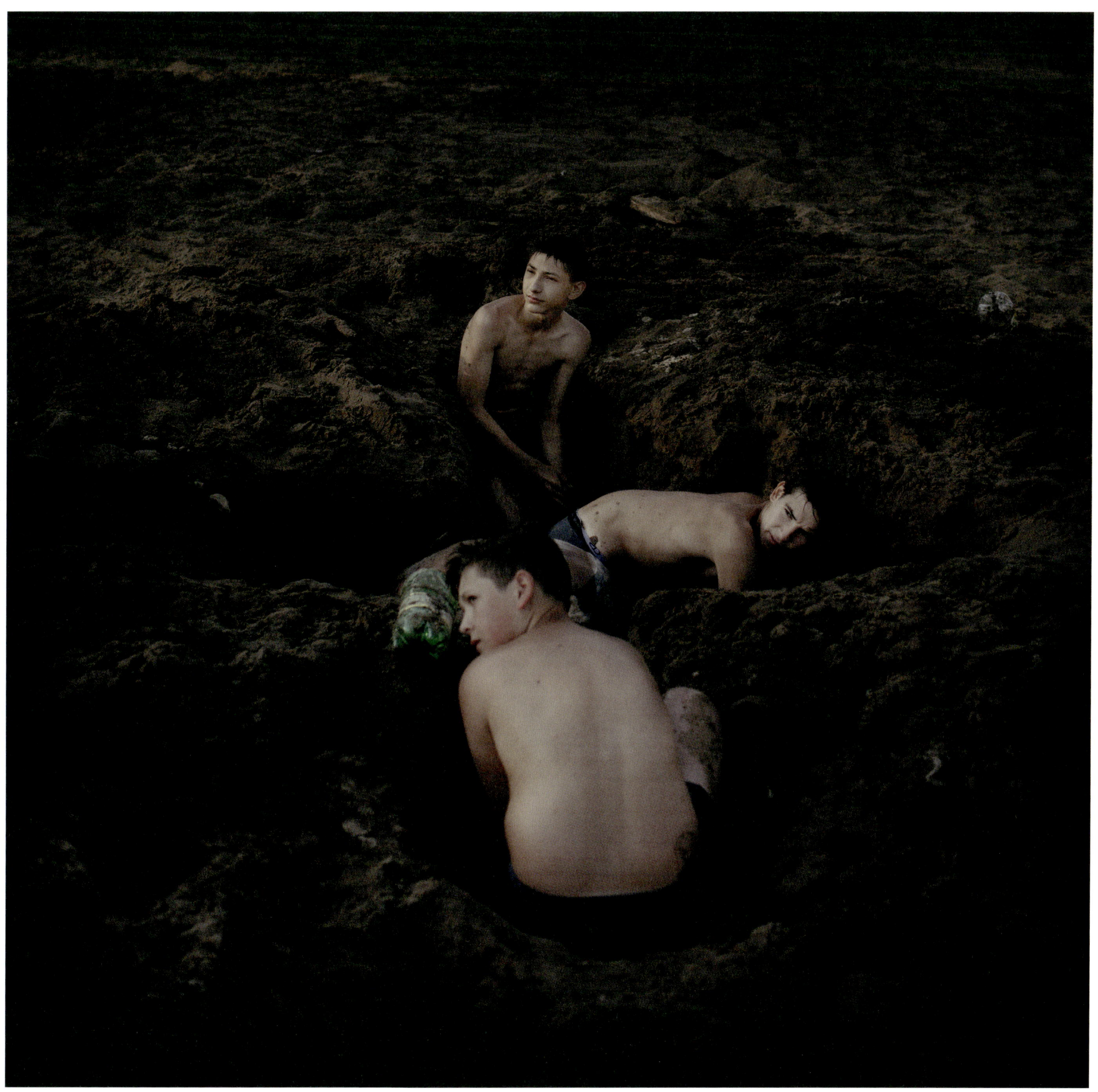

Vadul lui Vodă 2015

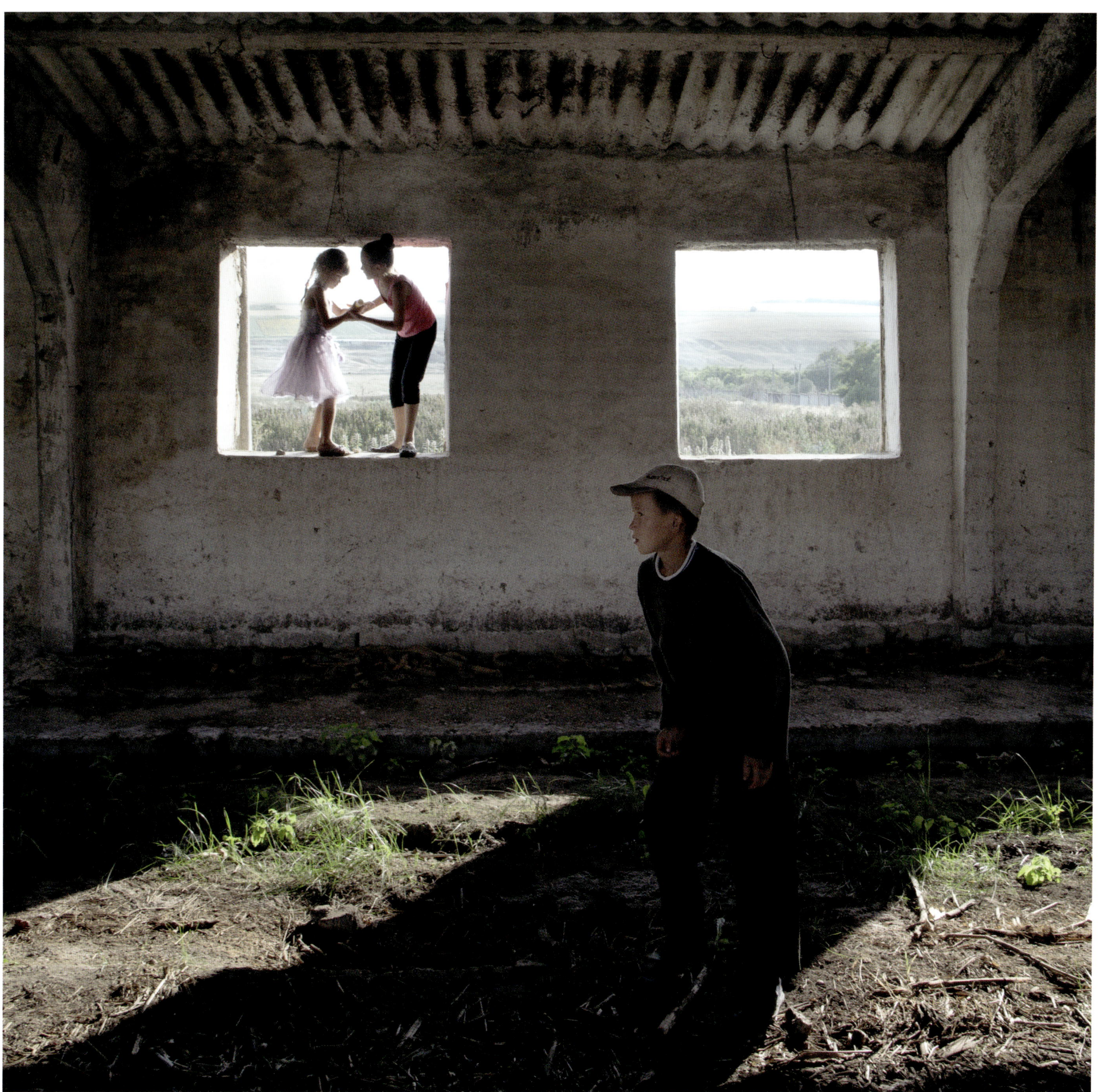

Kristina, Maria and Beniamin in an abandoned Kolkhoz, Chetrosu 2015

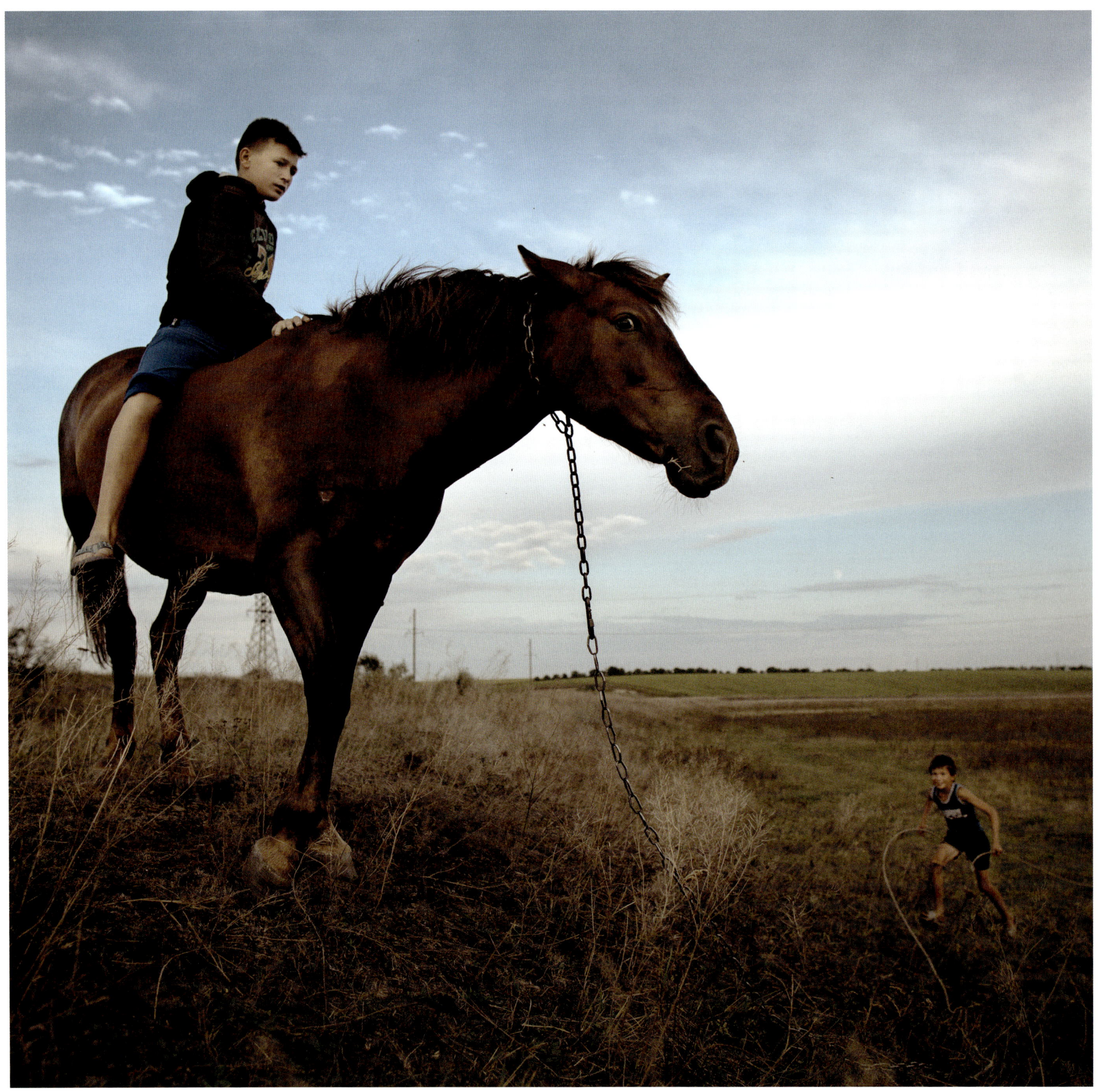

Iosif and Beniamin, Chetrosu 2016

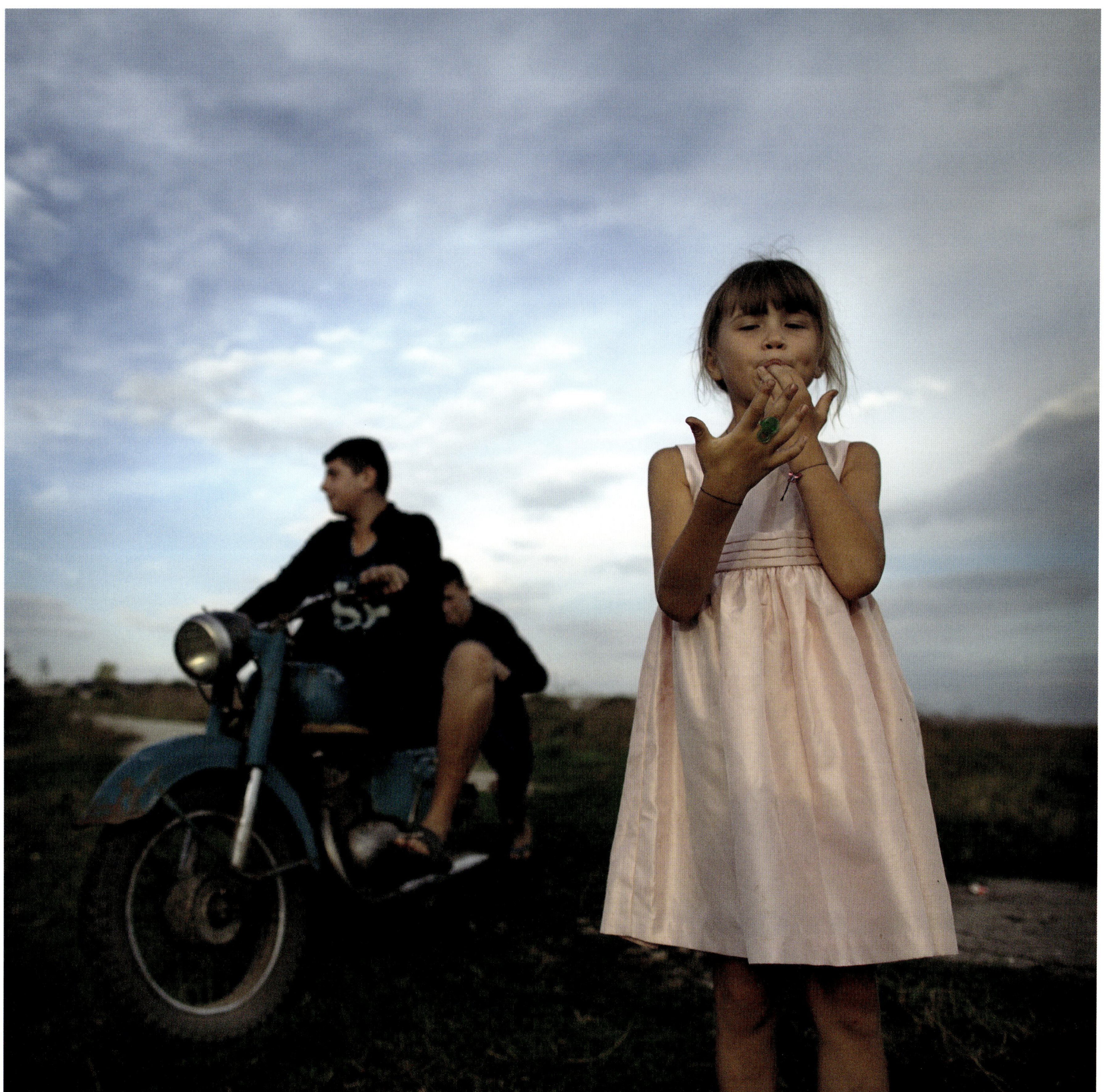

Kristina, Chetrosu 2016

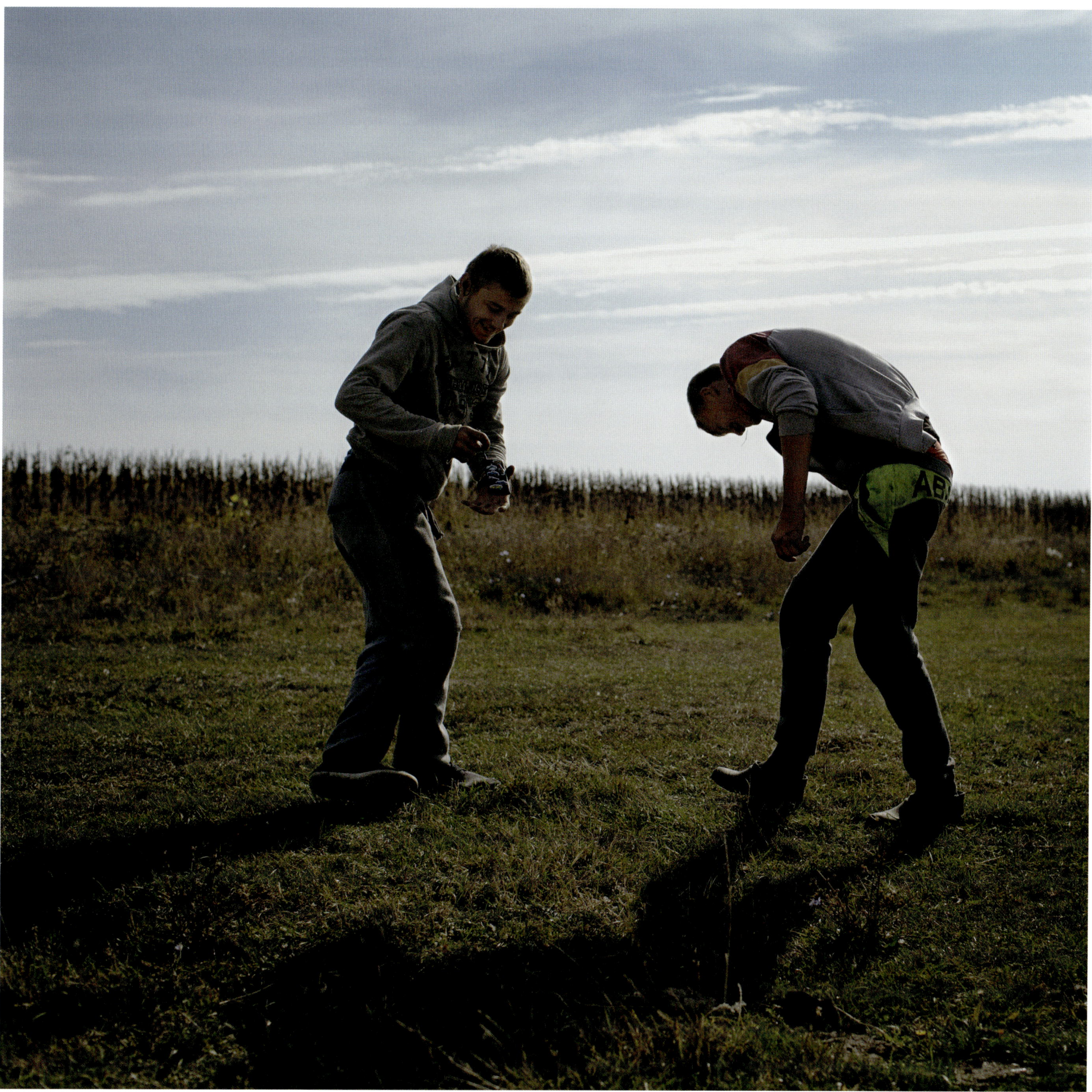

Ion and Mihail, Chetrosu 2016

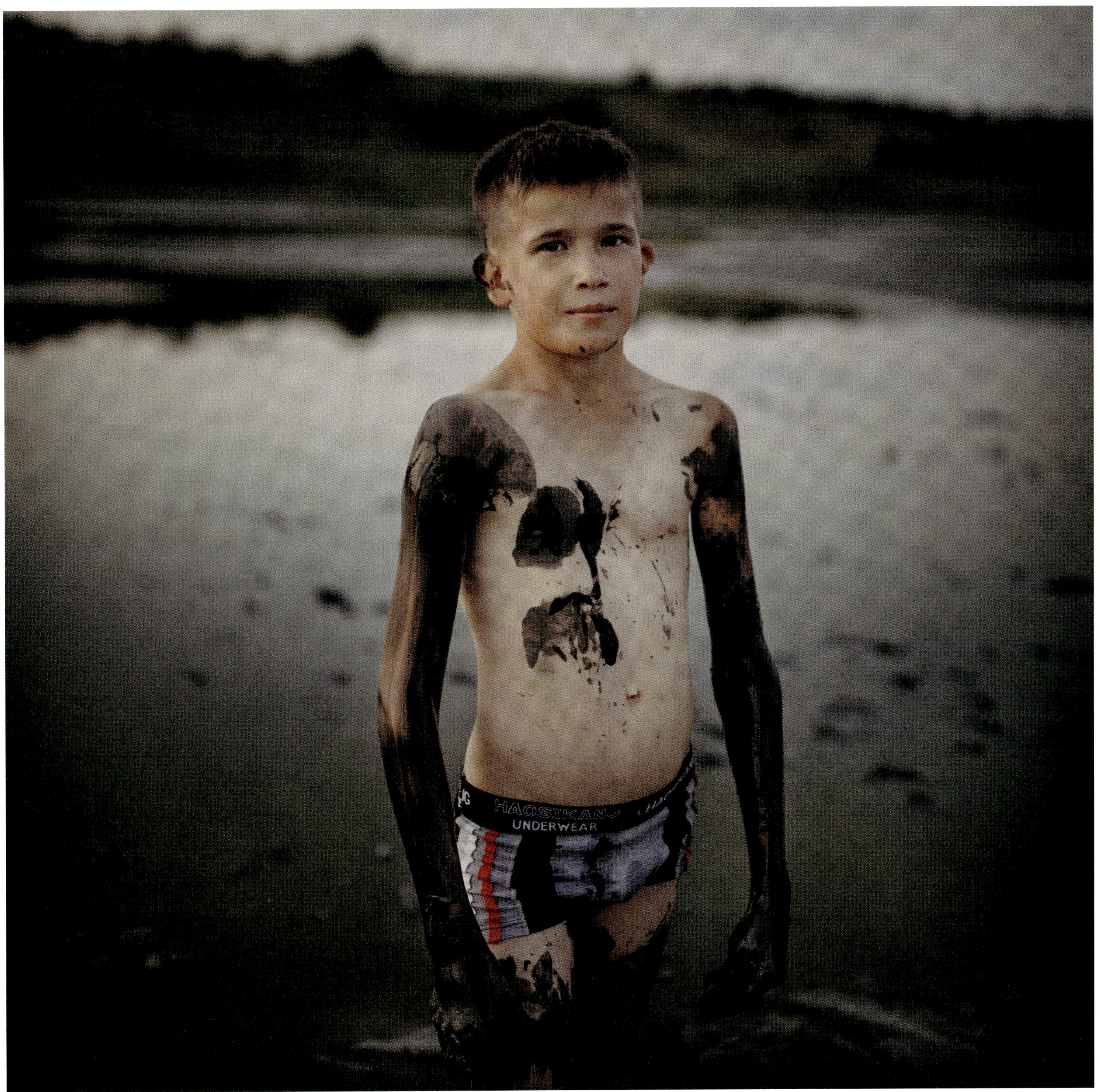

Beniamin, Chetrosu 2017

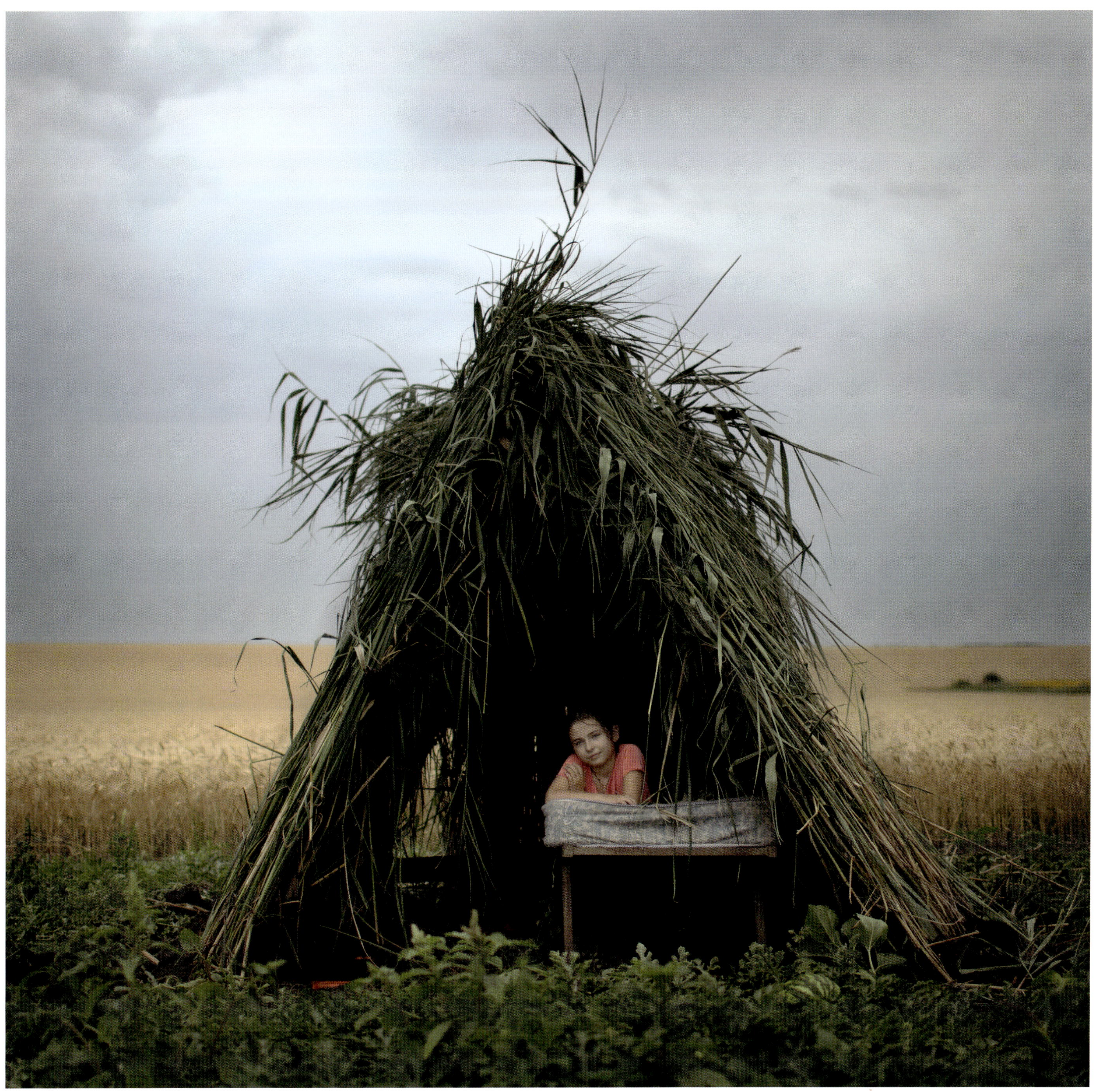

Shield on a watermelon field, Moldova 2015

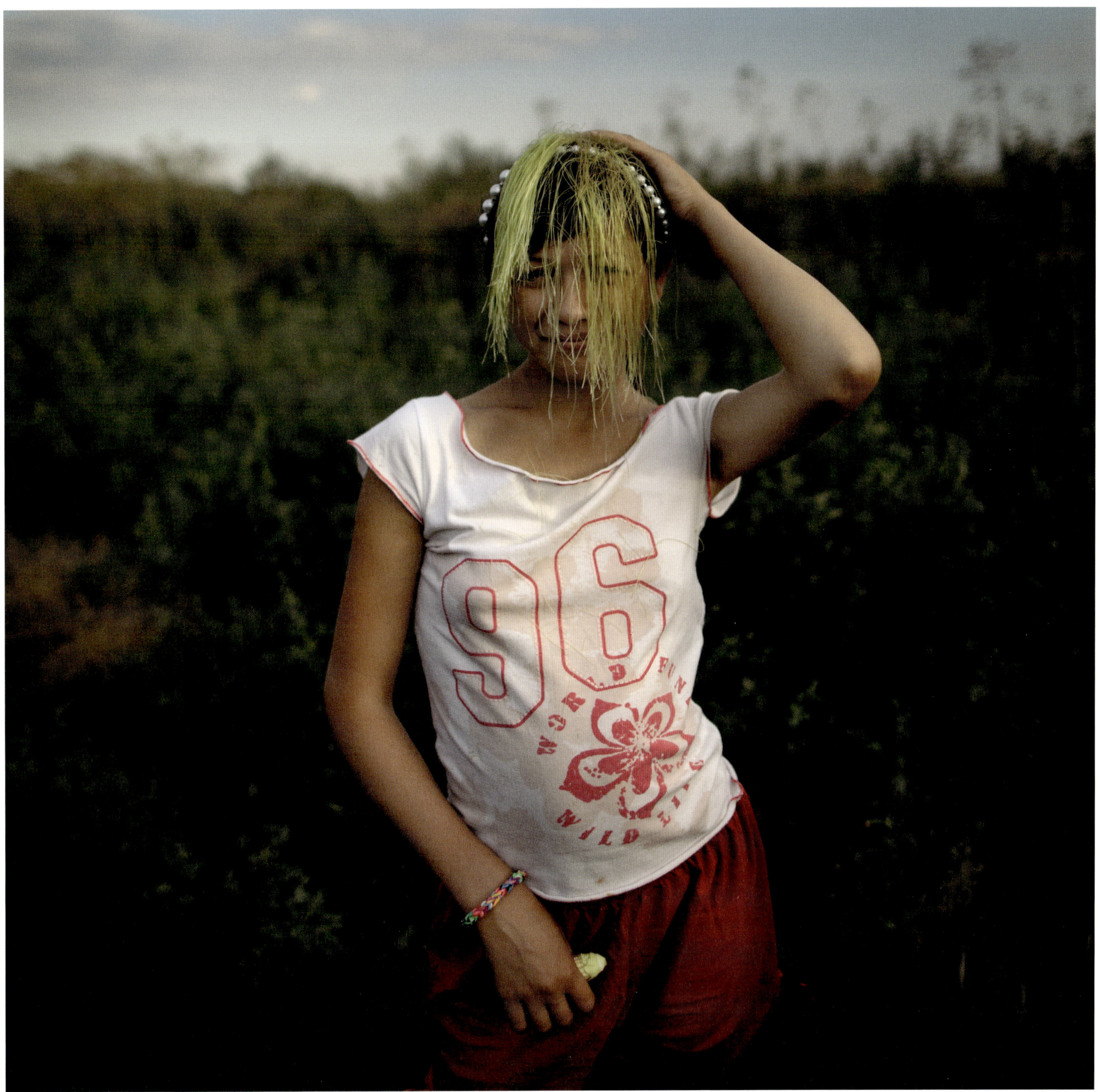

Maria, Chetrosu 2017

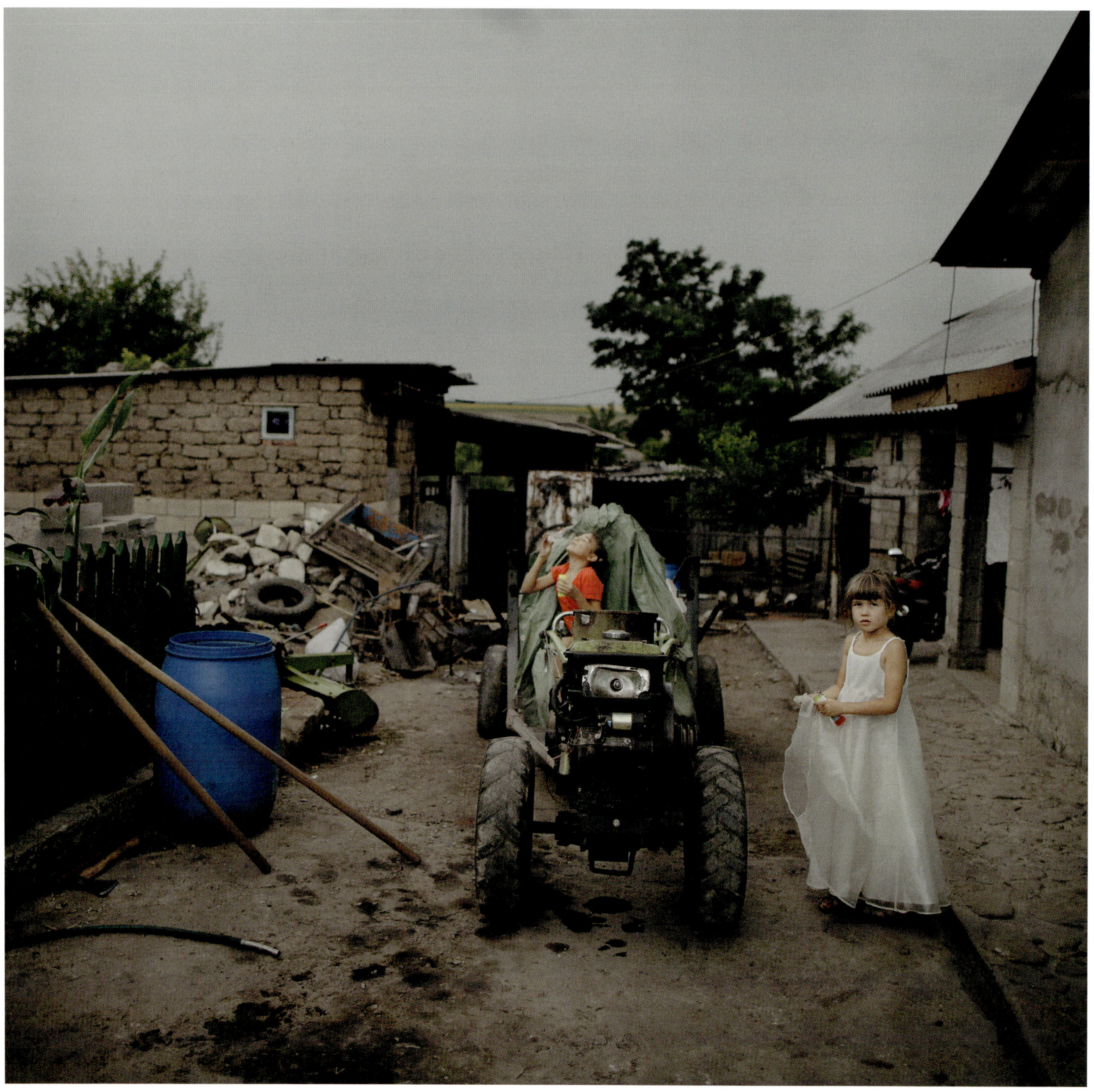

Maria and Kristina, Chetrosu 2014

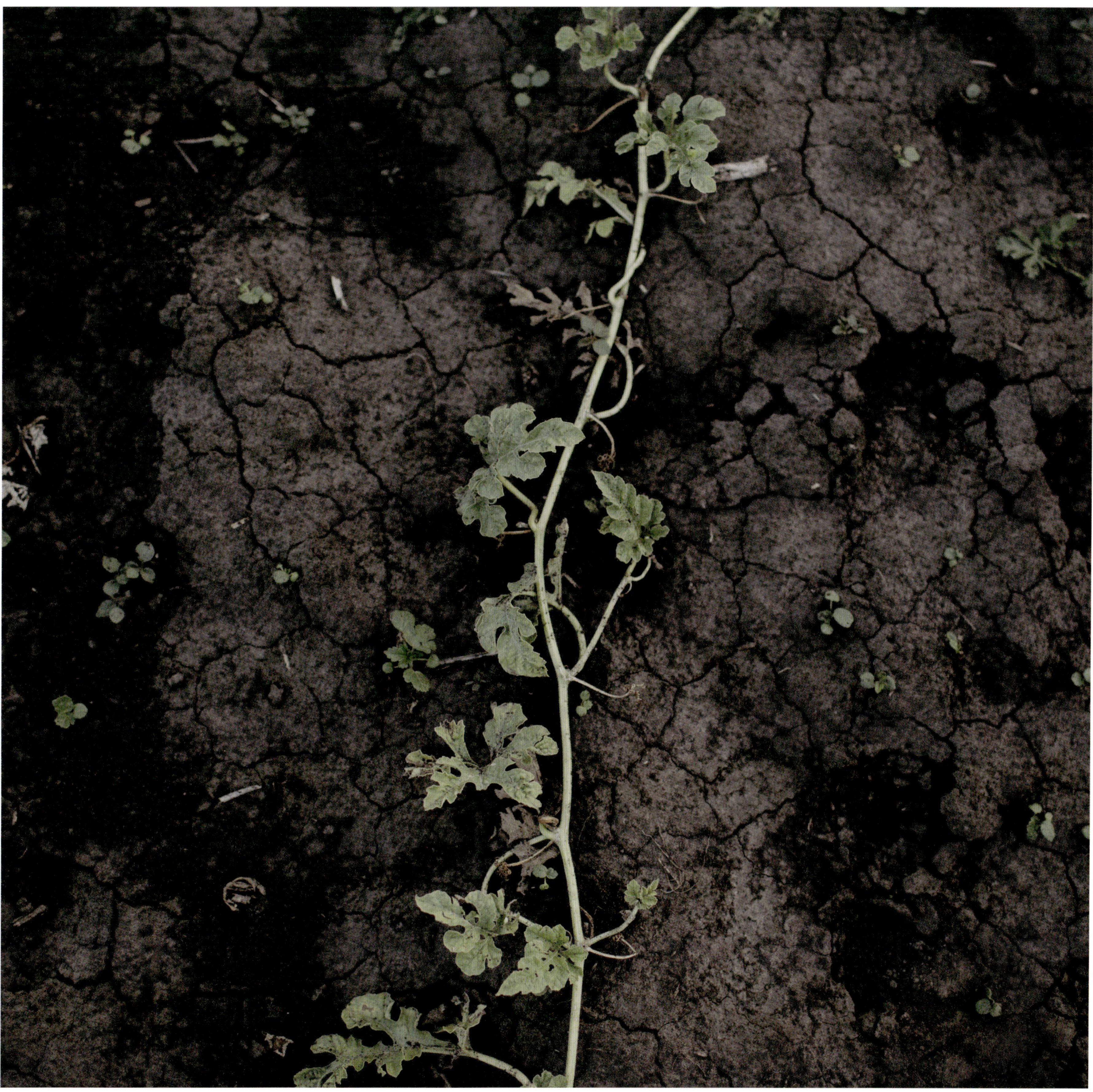

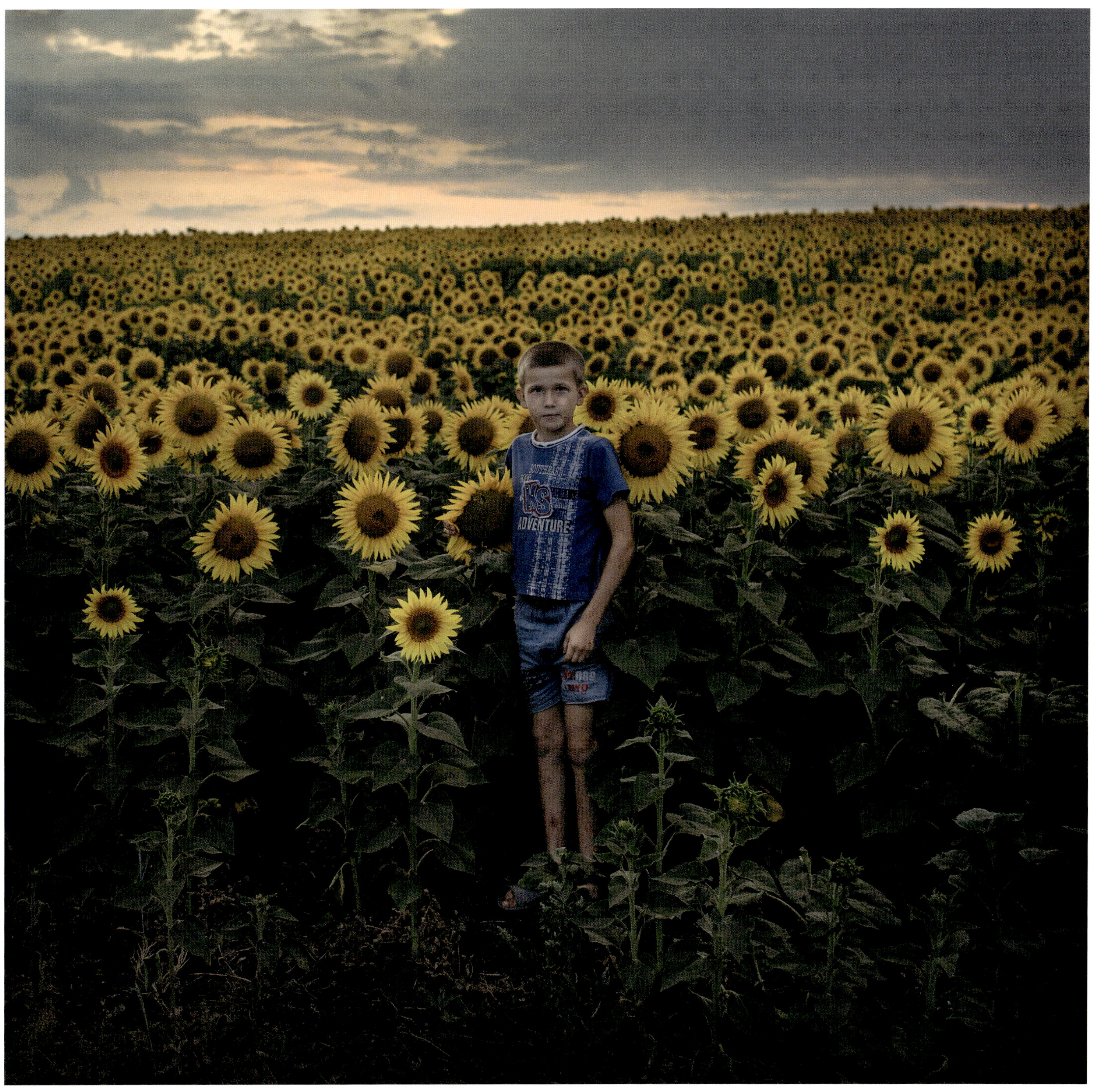

Beniamin, Chetrosu 2015

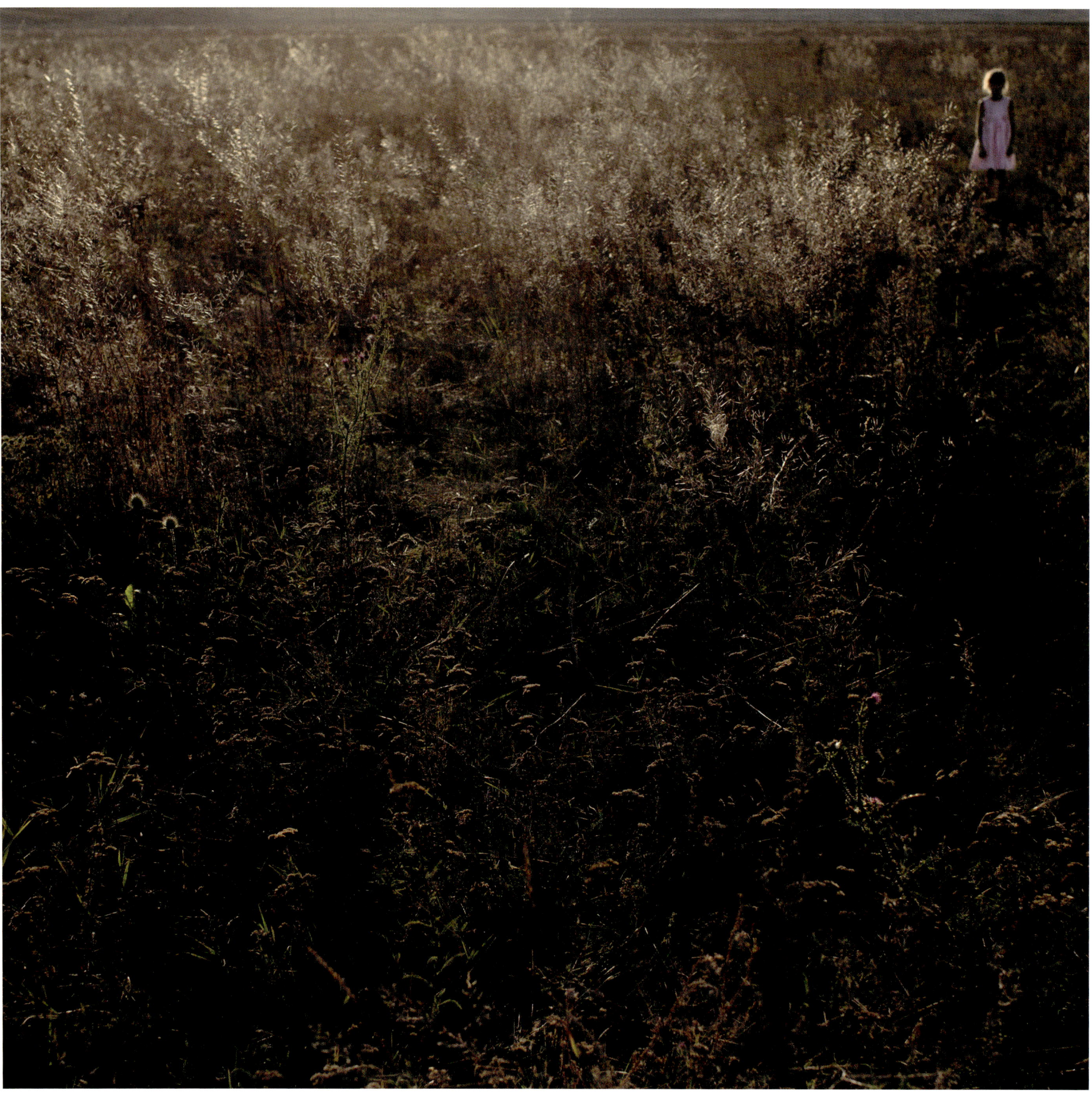

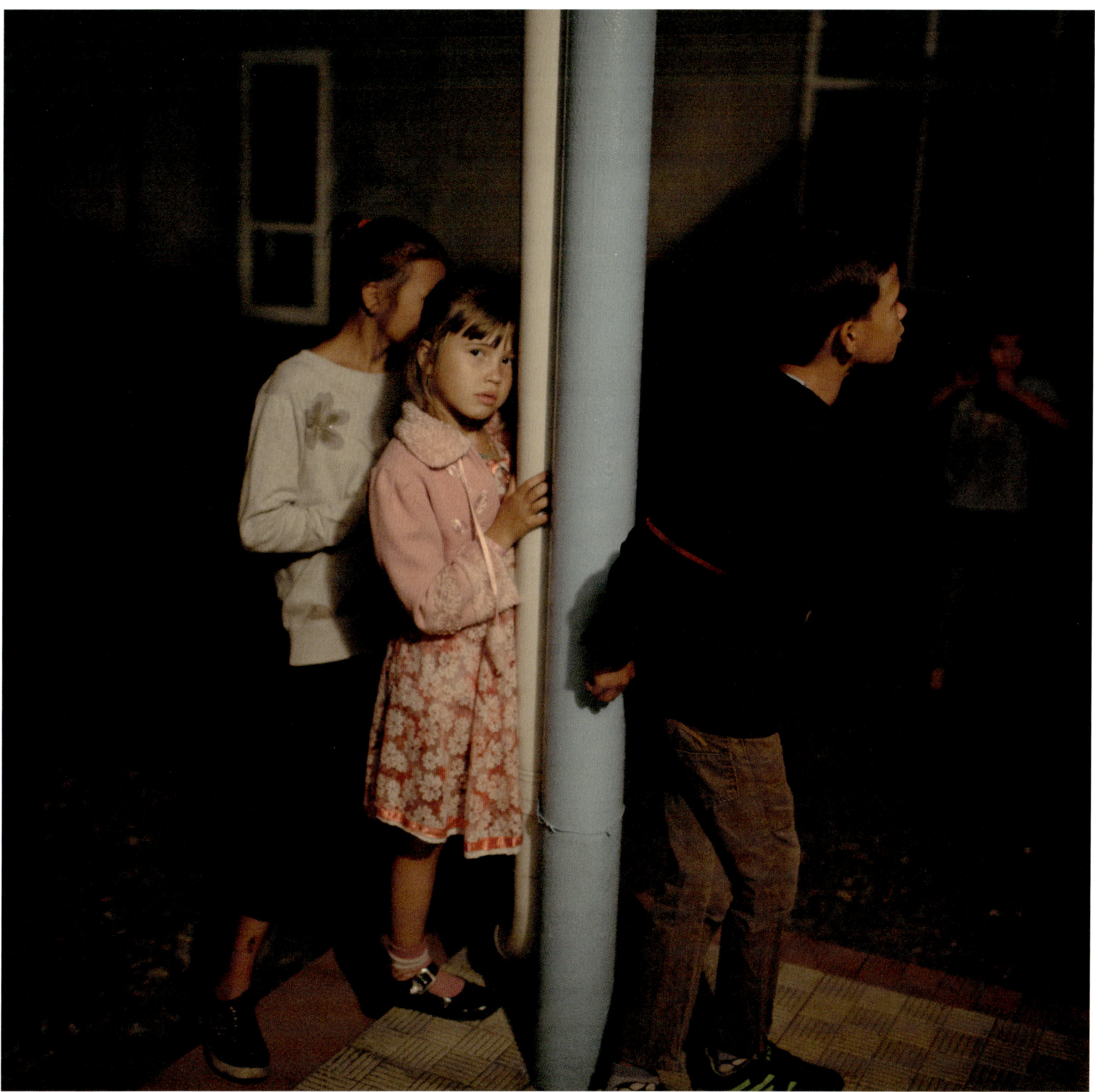

Kristina, Chetrosu 2016

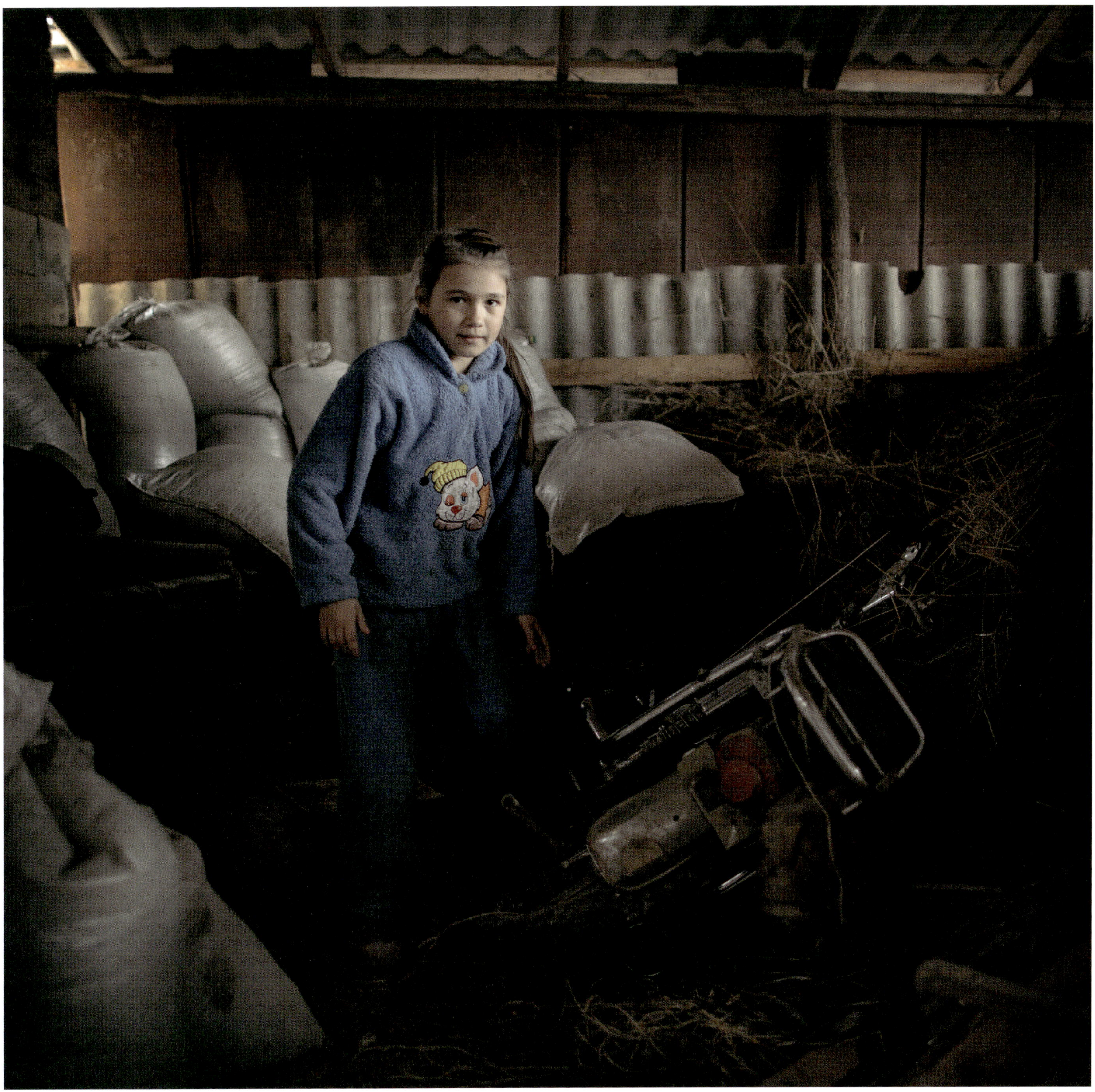

Maria, Chetrosu 2014

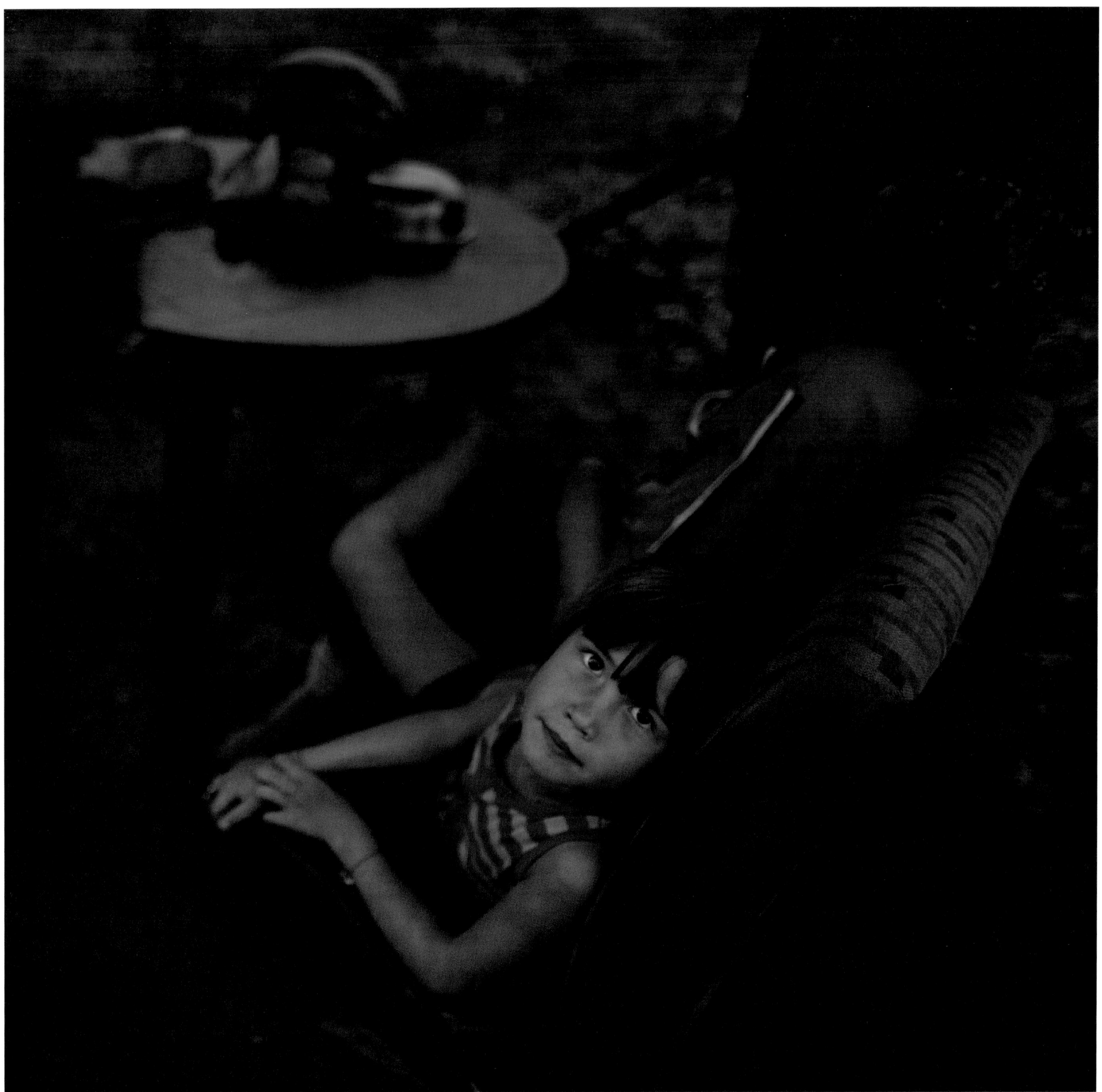

Kristina, Chetrosu 2016

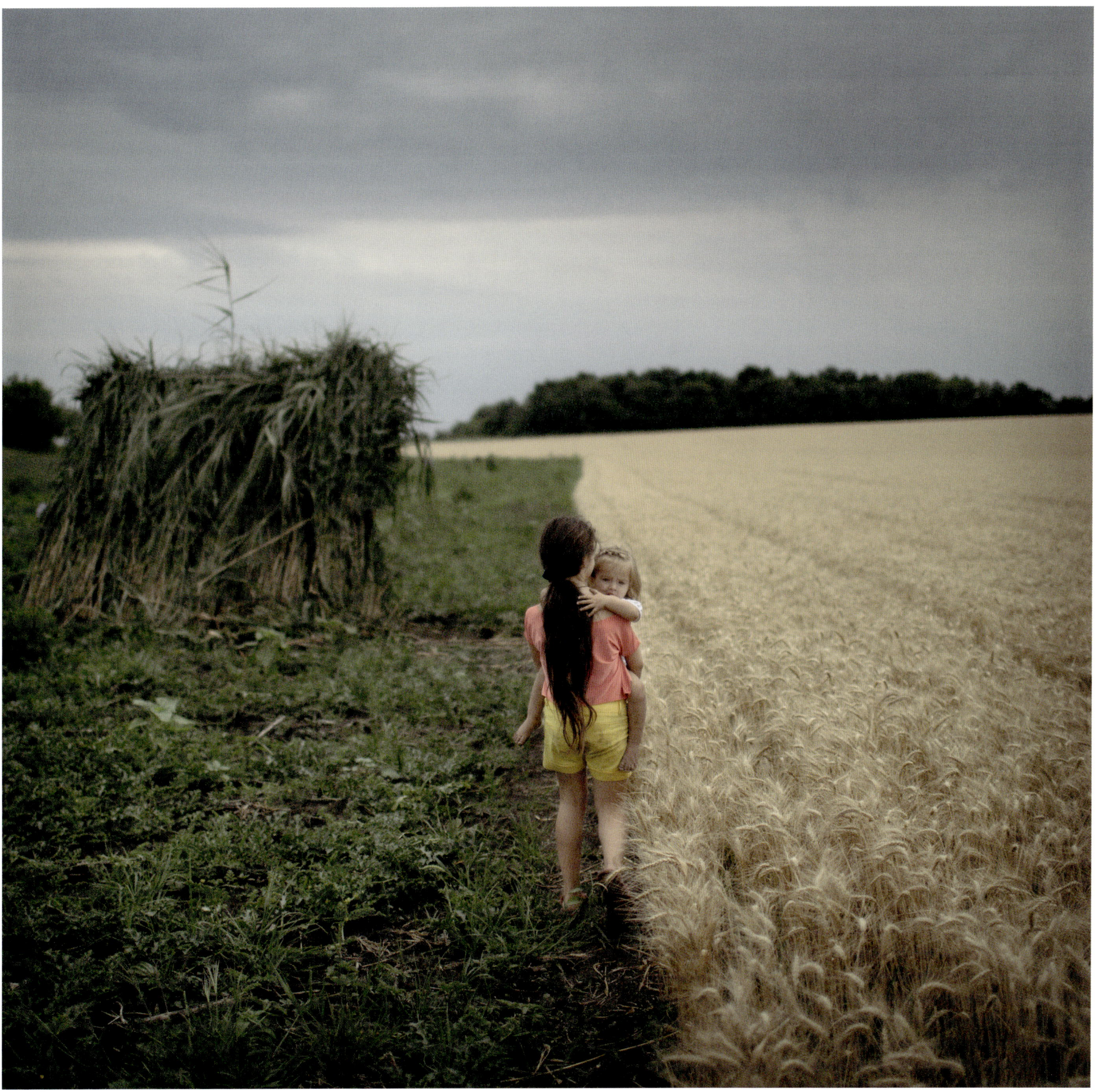

Moldova 2015

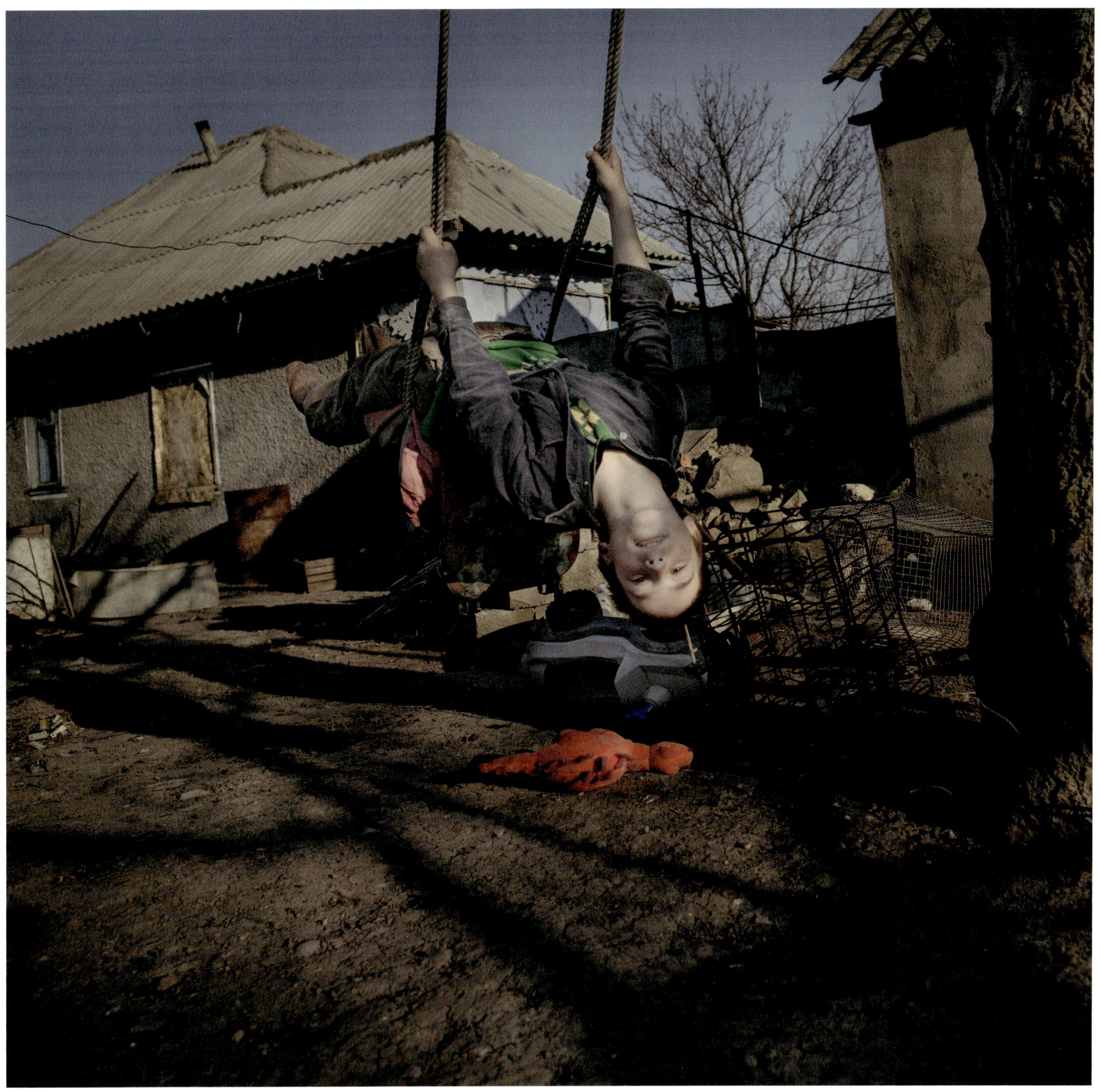

Igor, Baroncea 2014

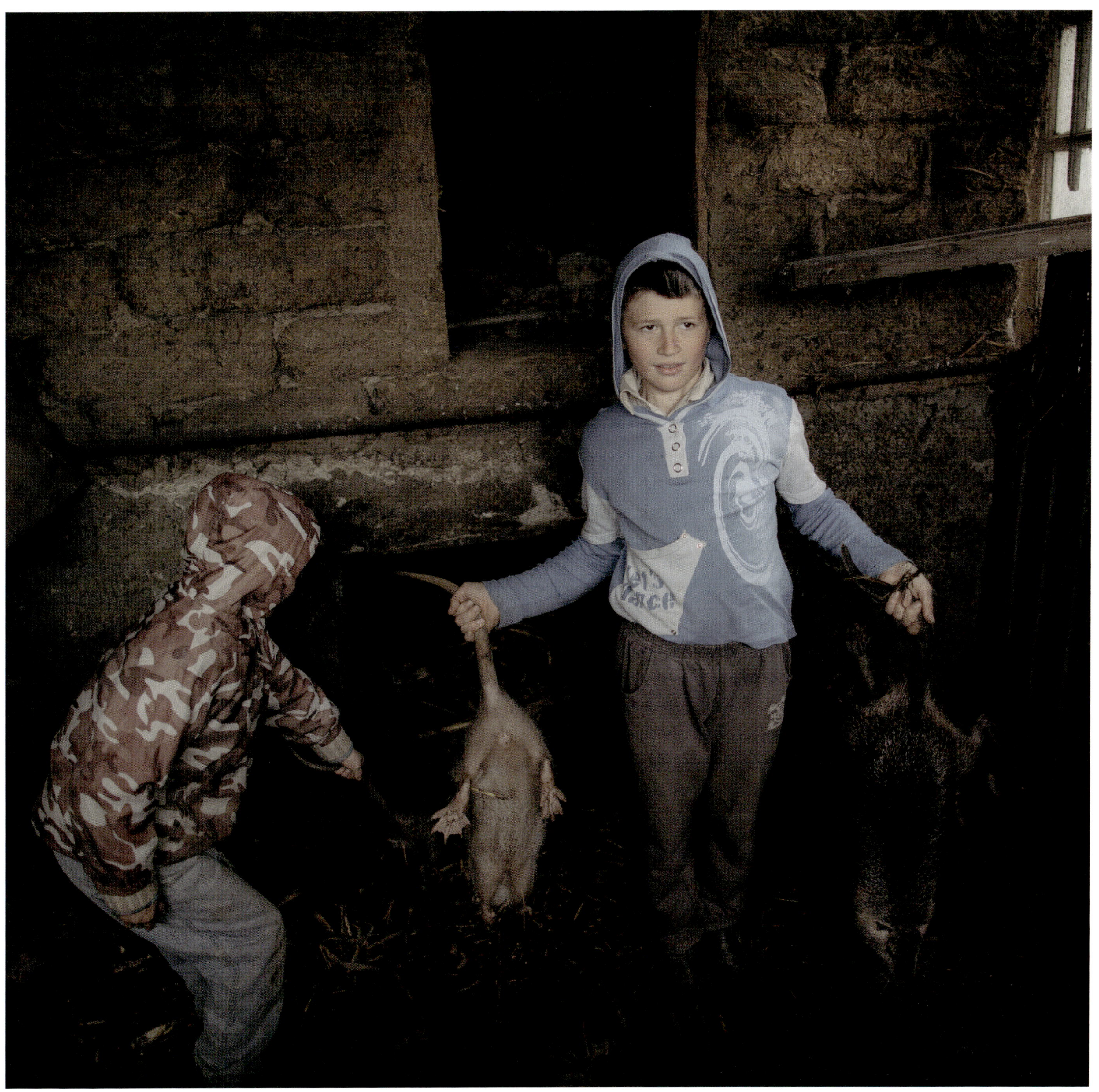

Beniamin and Iosif, Chetrosu 2014

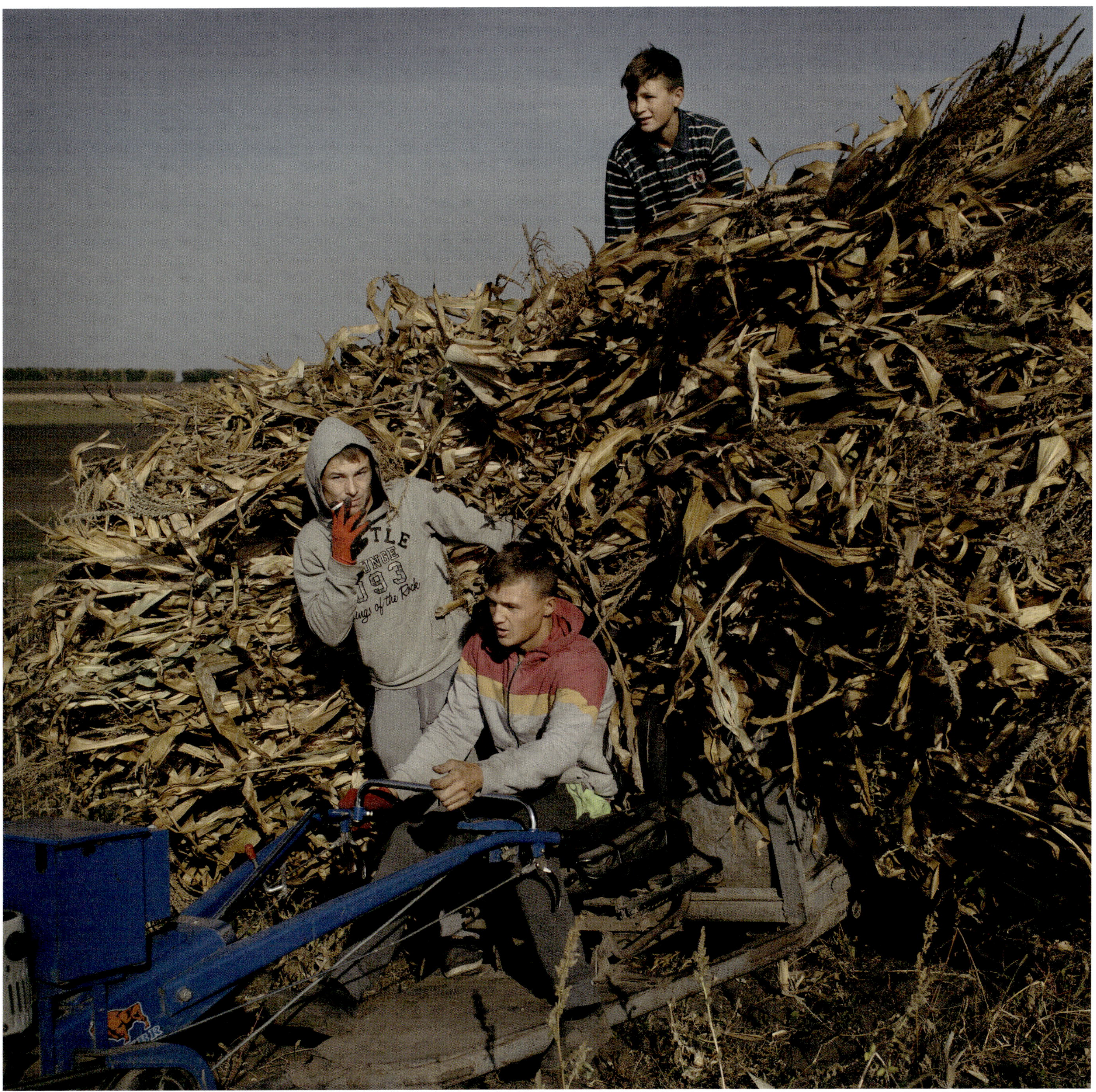

Ion, Mihail and Iosif, Chetrosu 2016

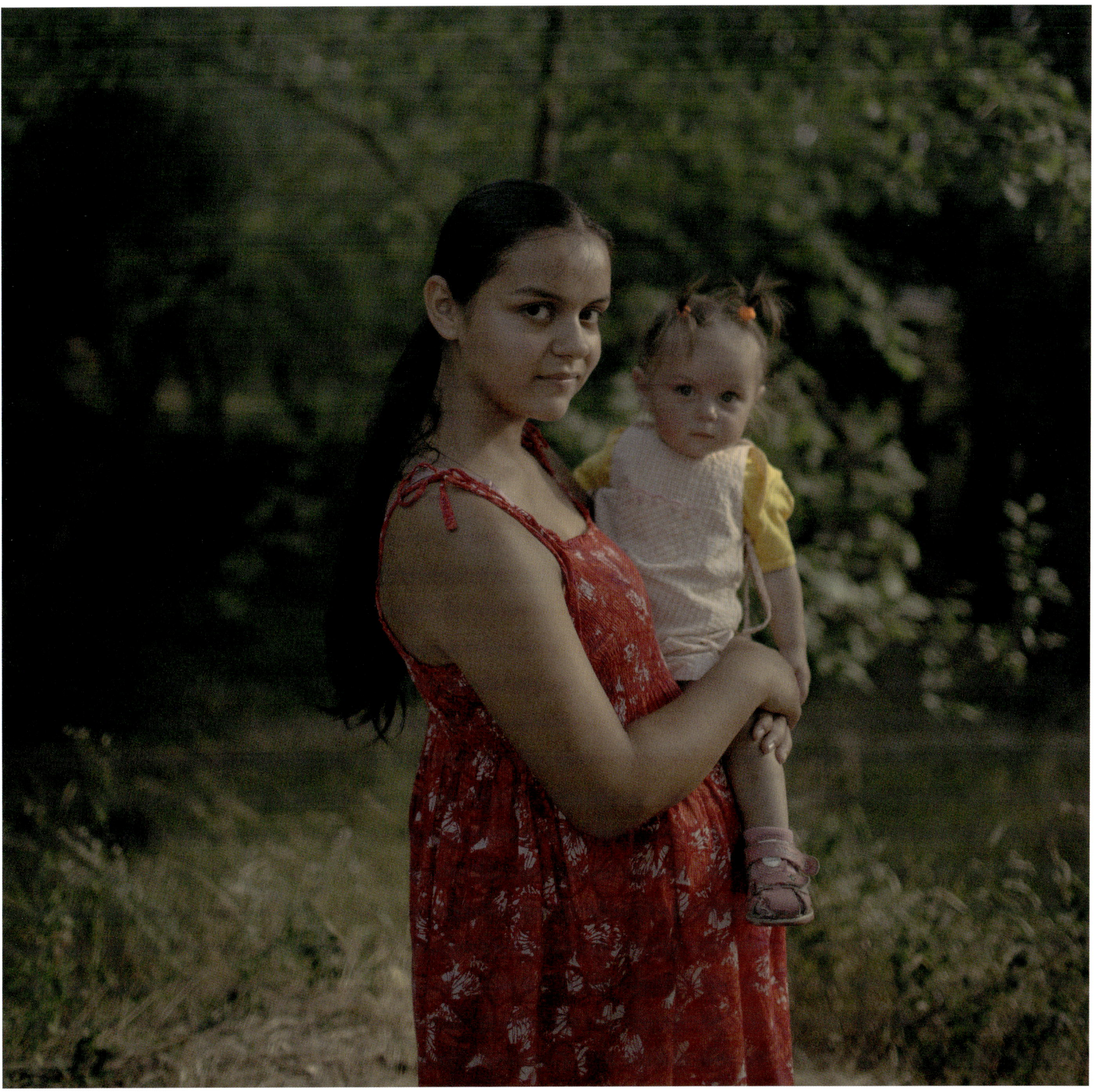

Young pregnant mother, Rîbnița Transnistria 2015

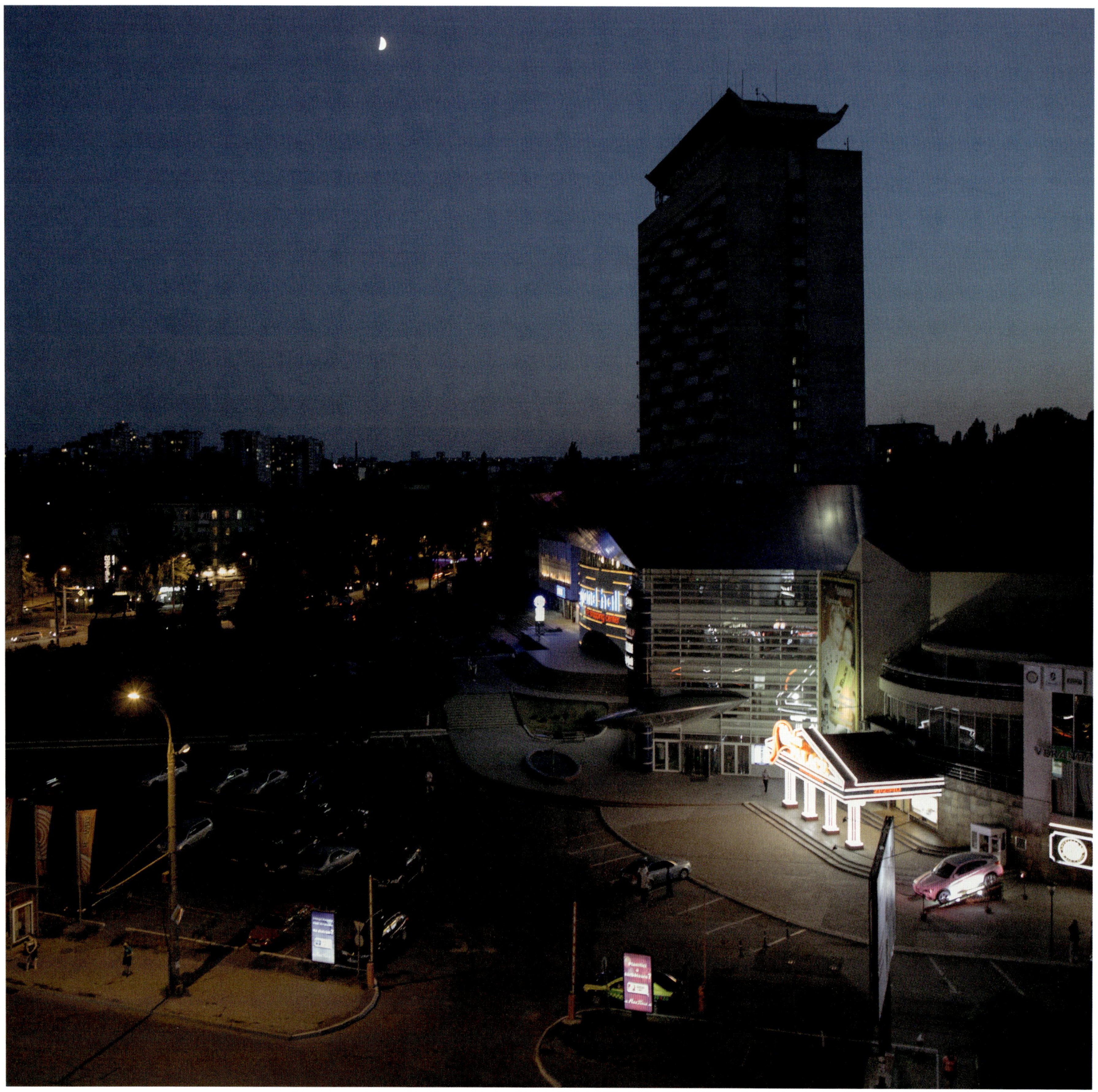

Chisinau 2015

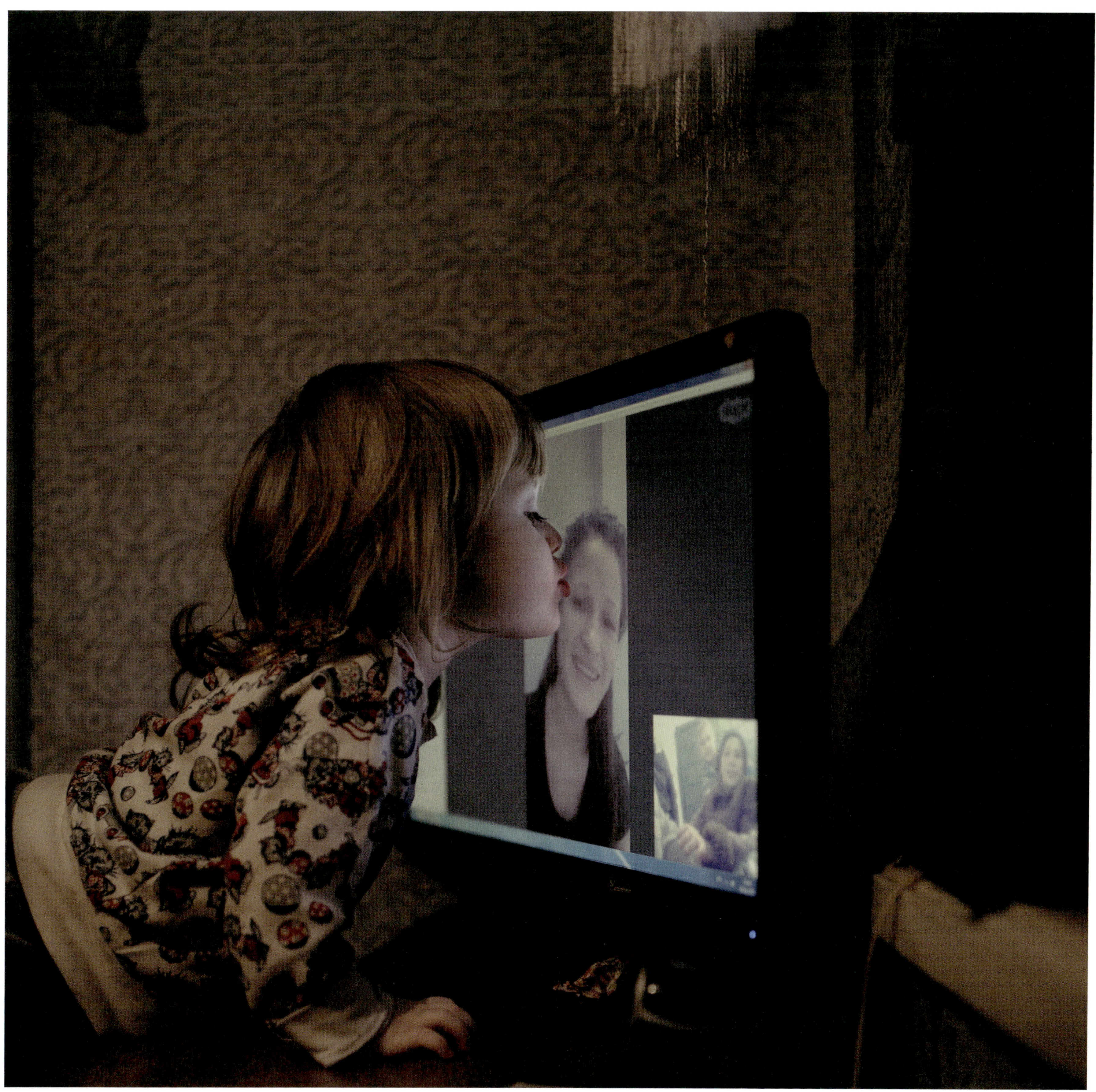

Little Kristina kisses her mother Ana on skype, Chetrosu 2017

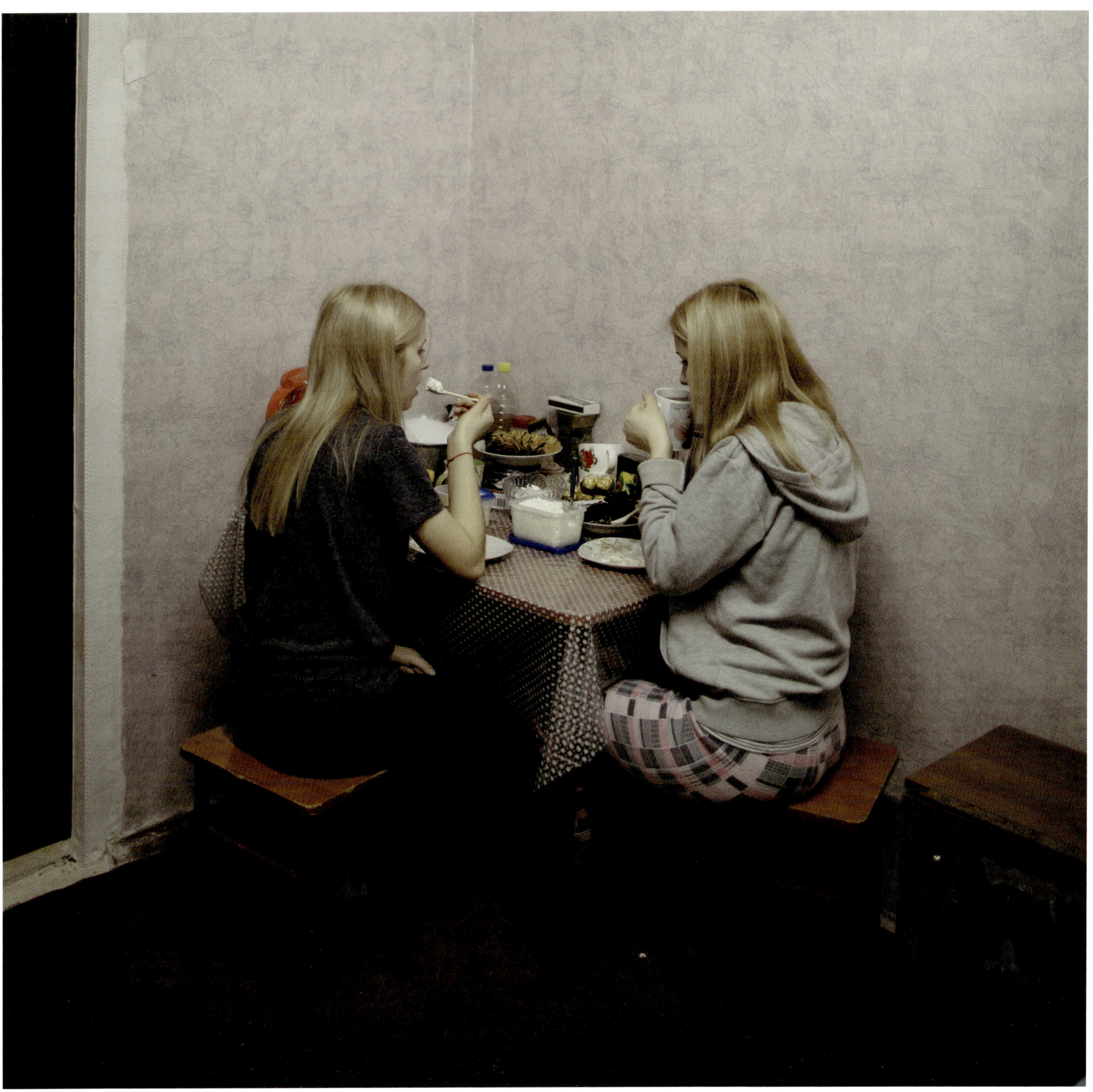

Mihaela and Kristina in their dormitory, Chisinau 2017

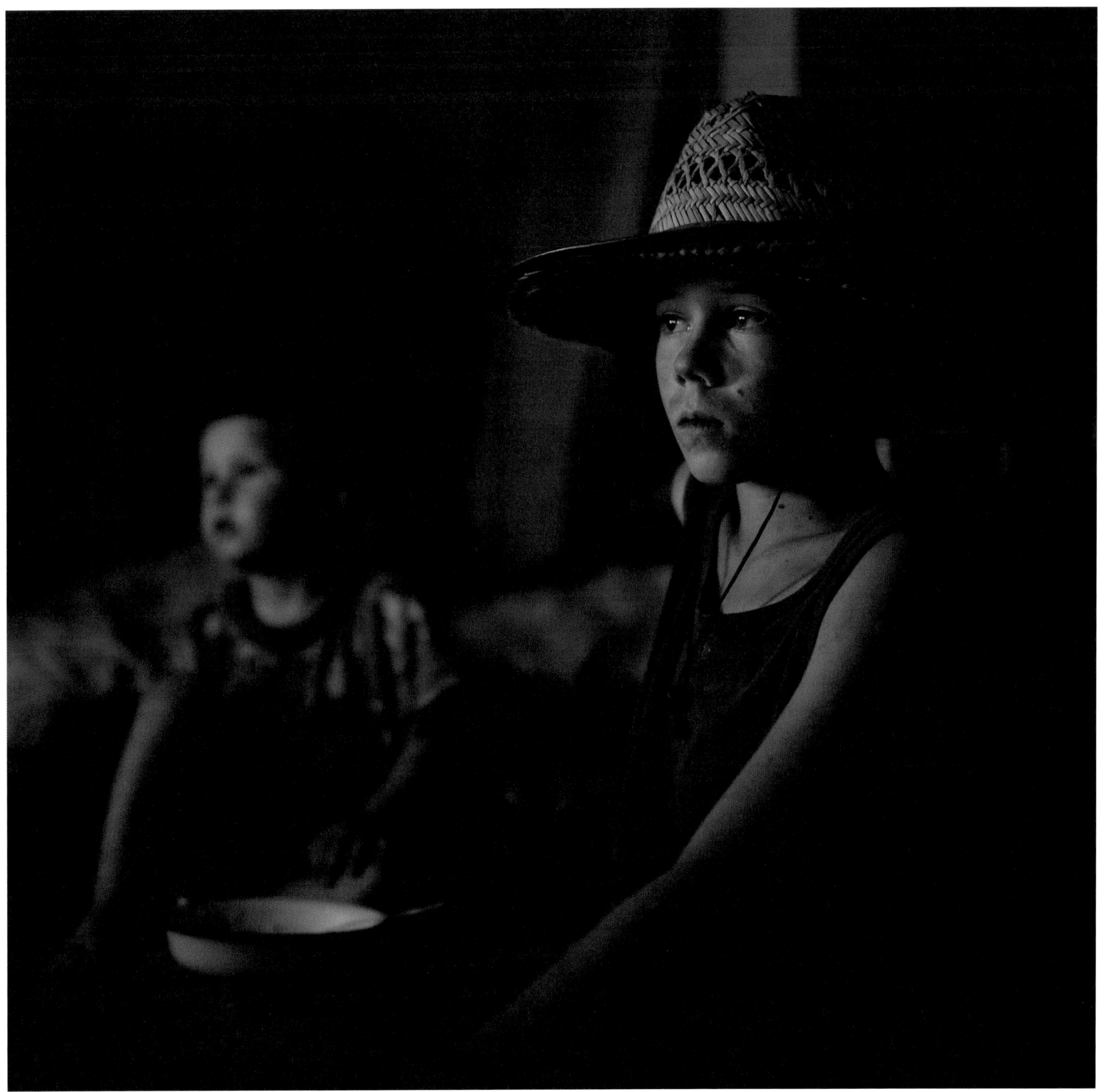

Aurel, Chetrosu 2016

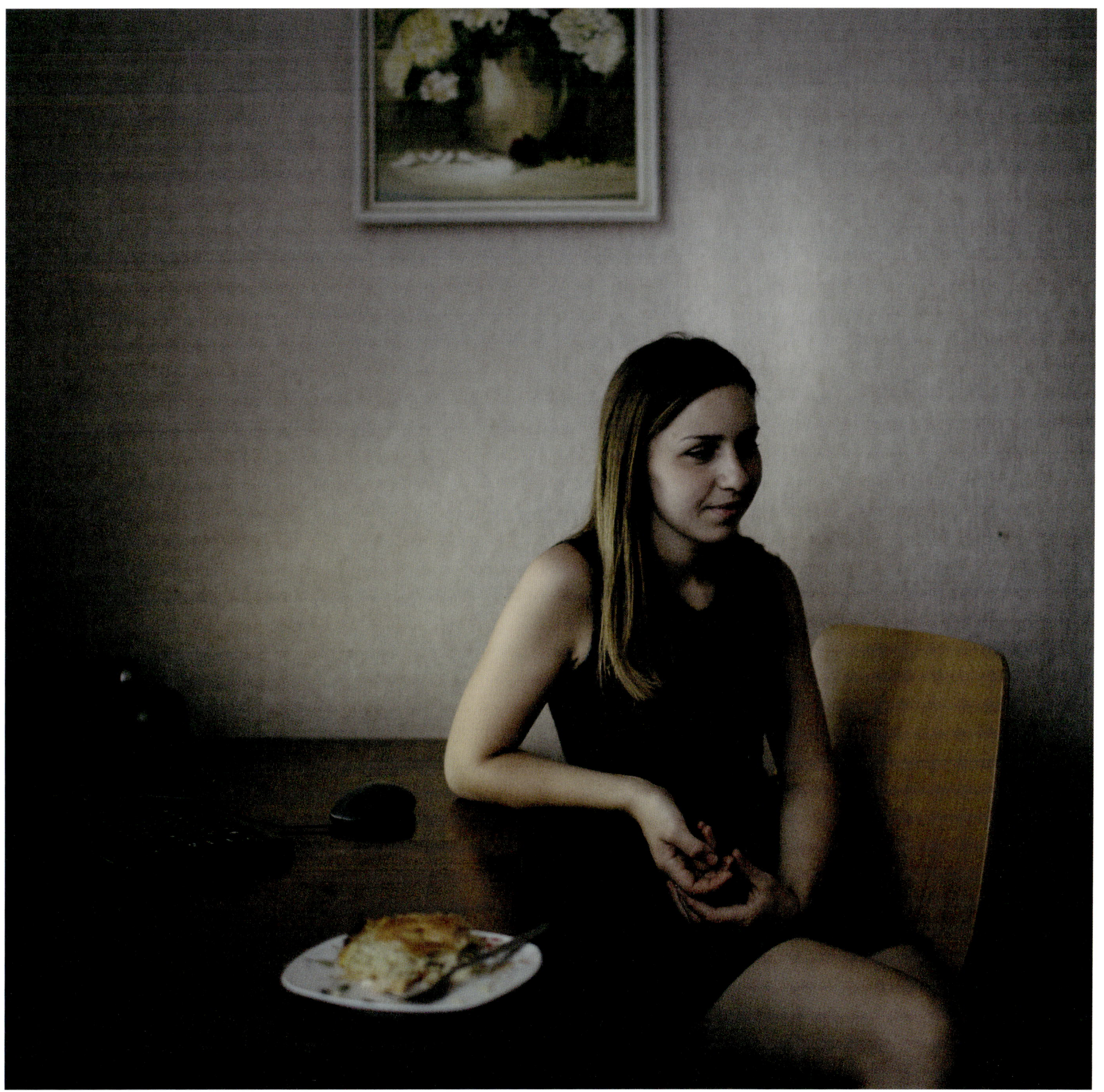

Karina, Doroțcaia 2016

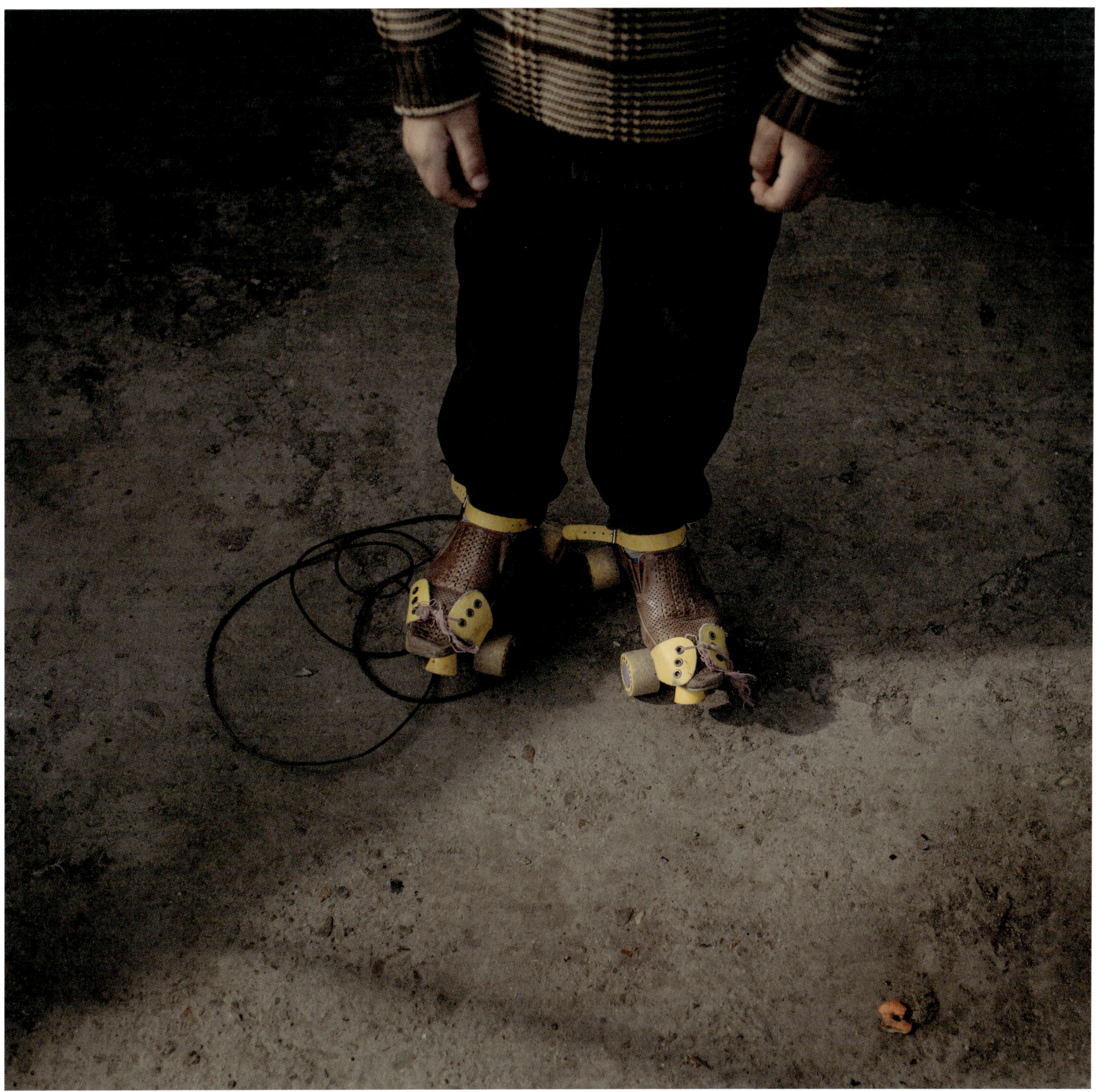

Baroncea 2014

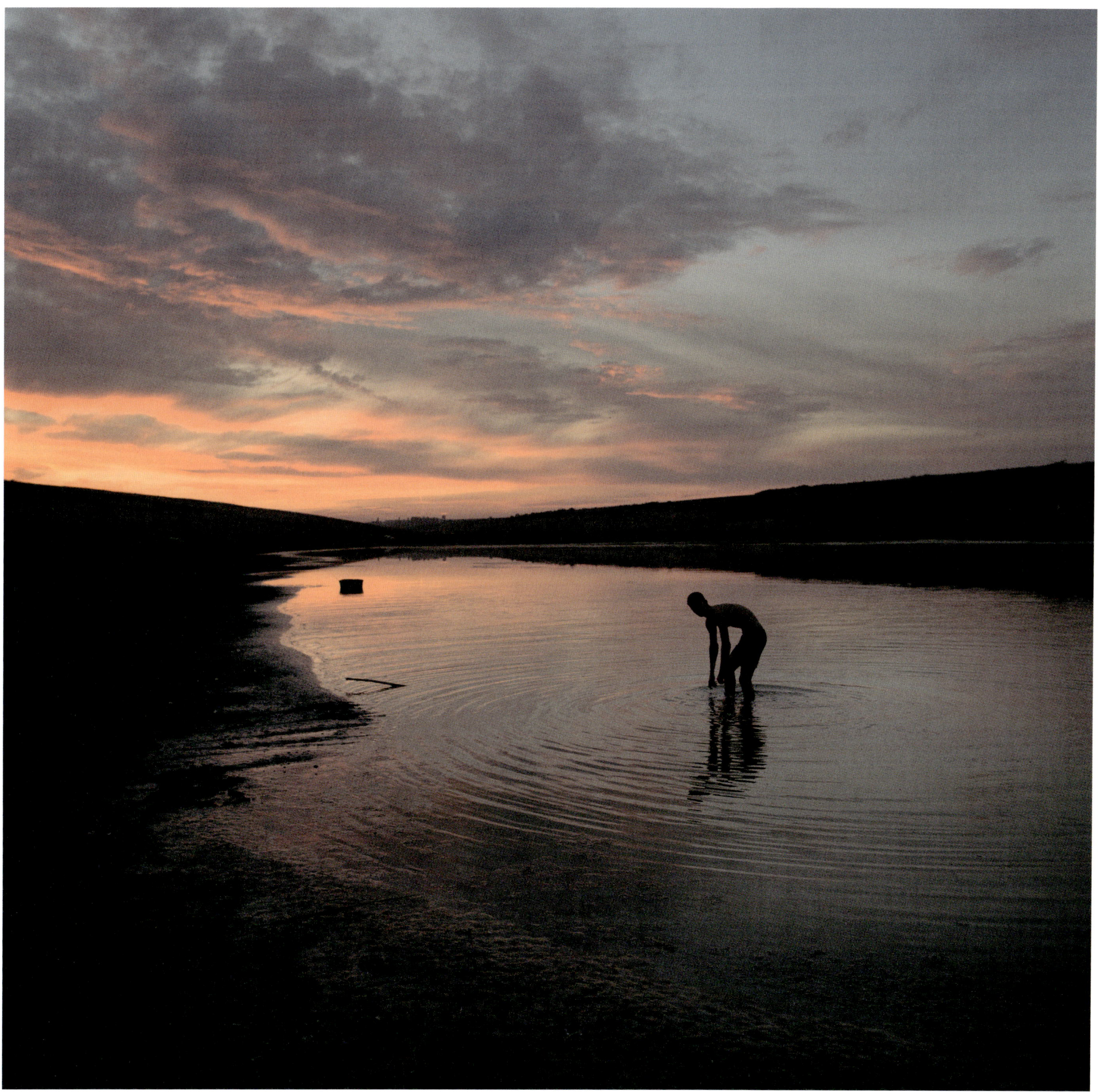

Mihail, Chetrosu 2016

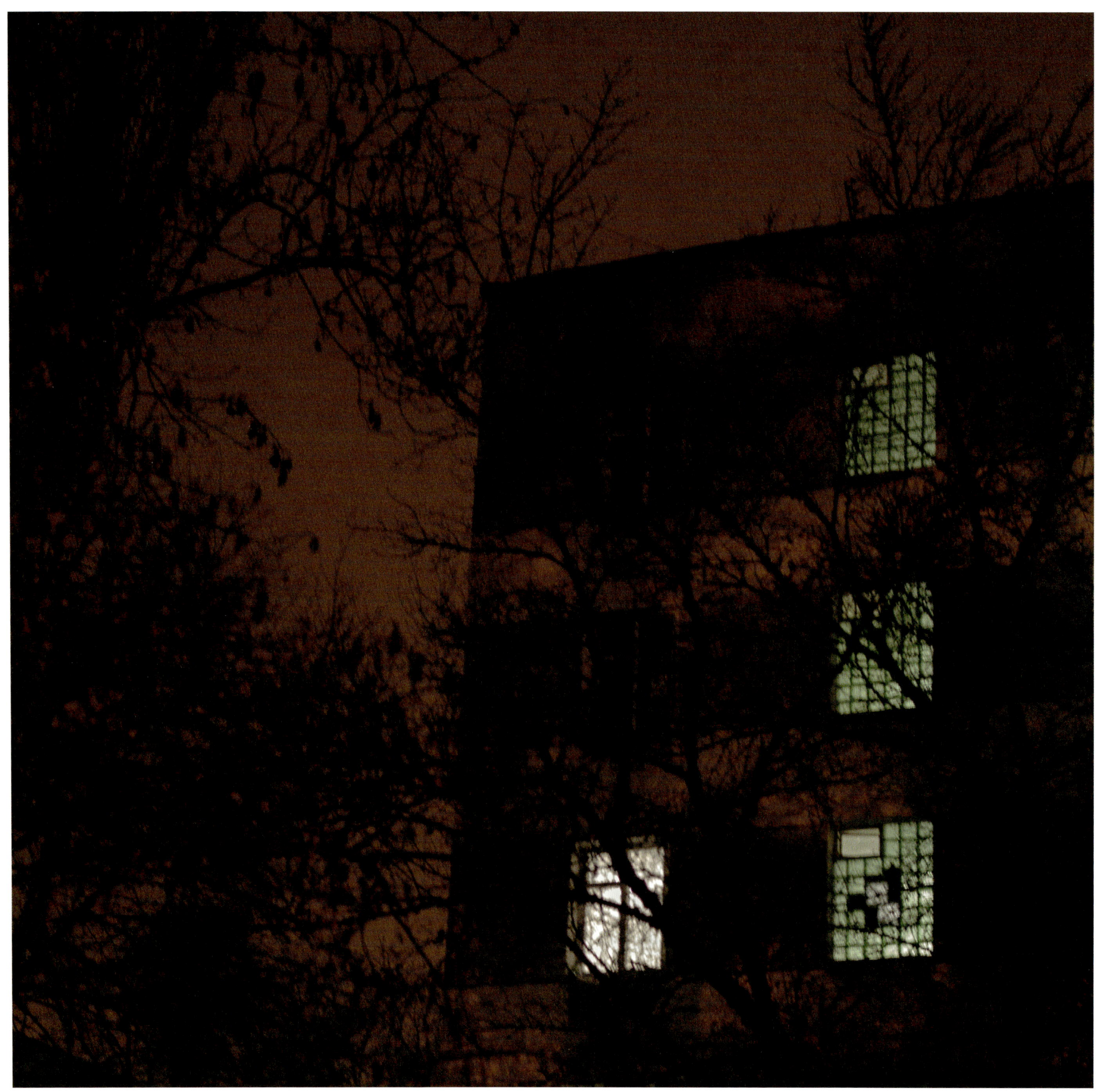

Dormitory, Chisinau 2017

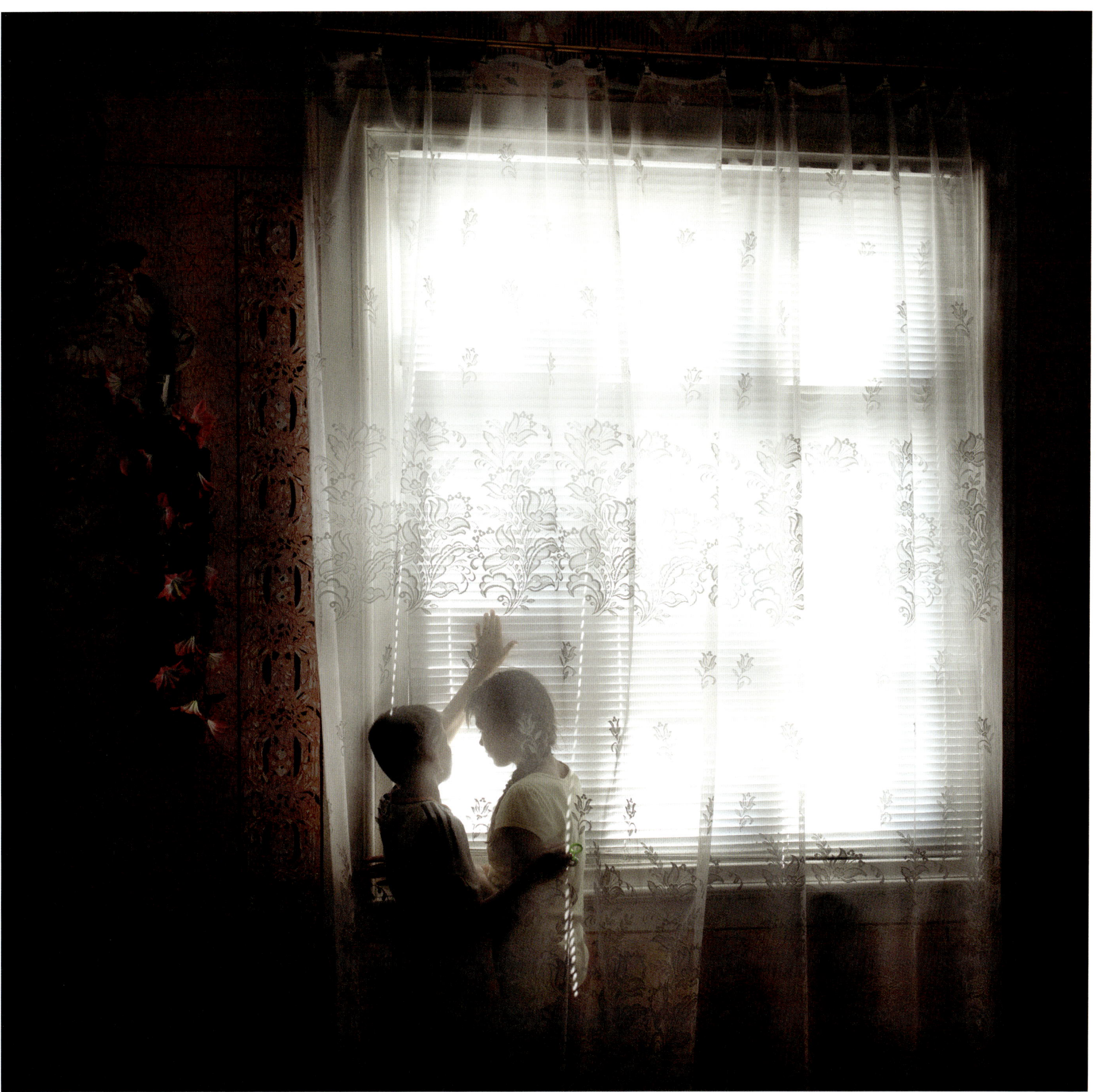

Beniamin and Maria, Chetrosu 2017

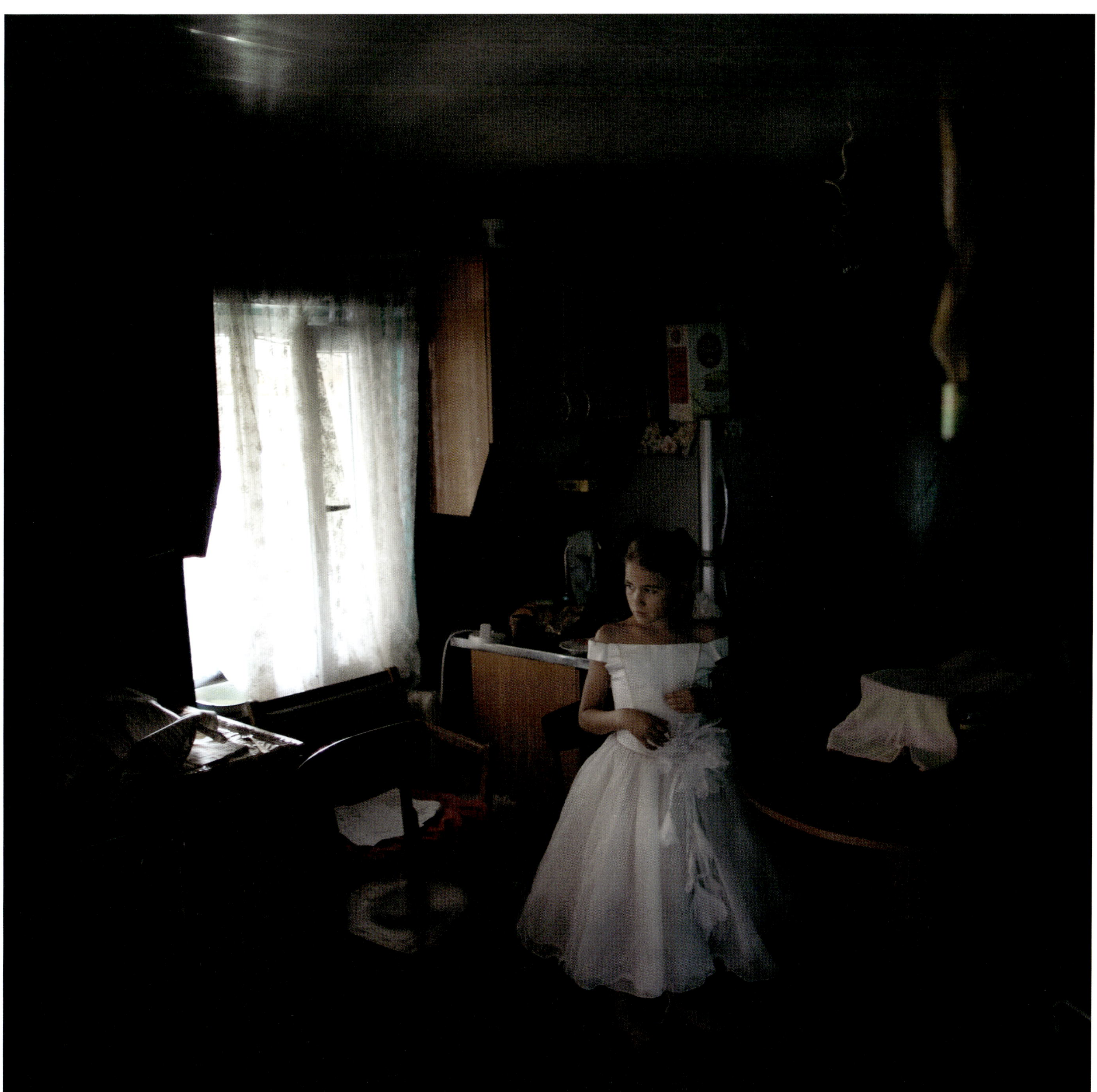

Maria, Chetrosu 2015

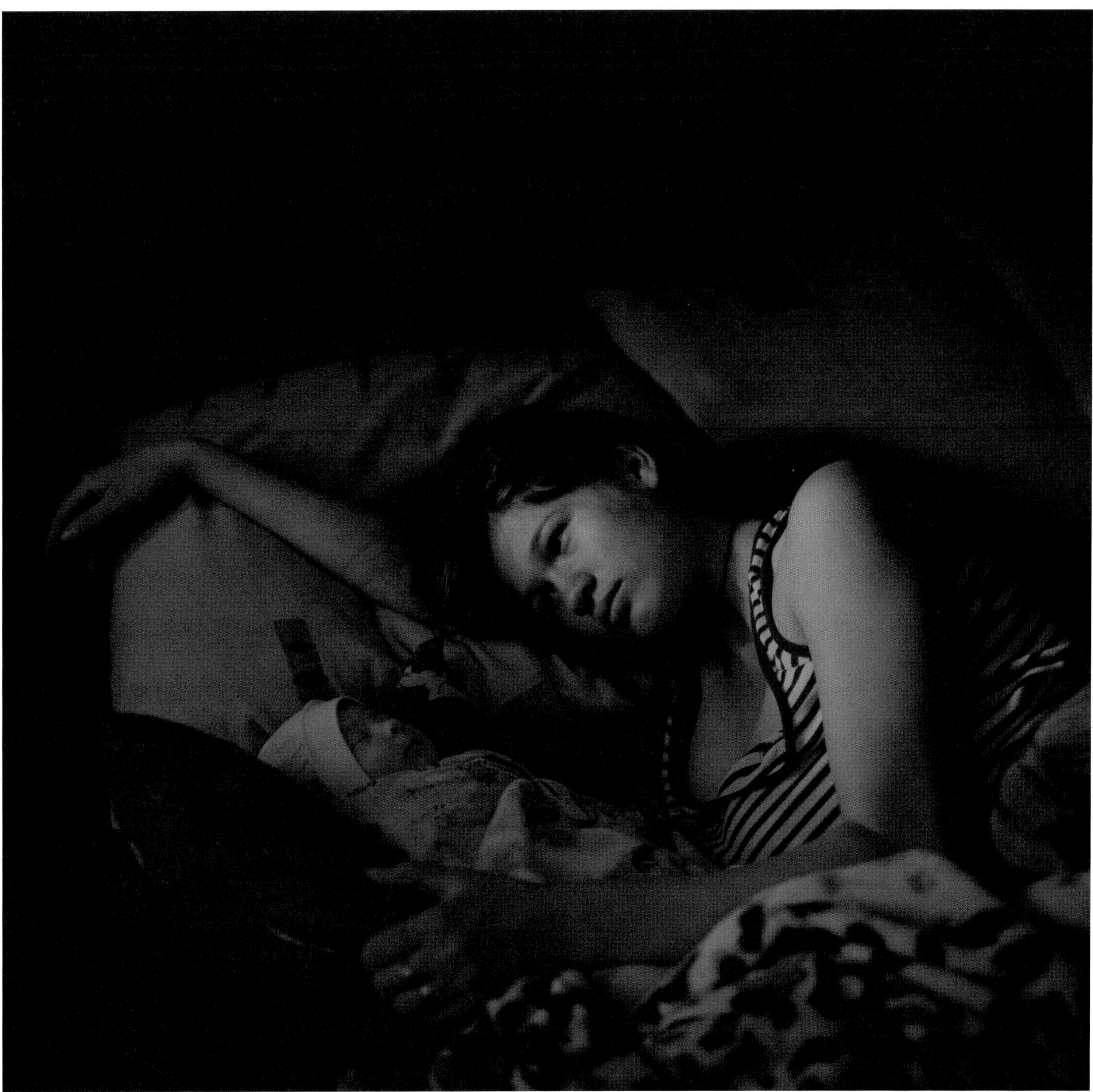

Natalia and her first born Anastacia, Chetrosu 2016

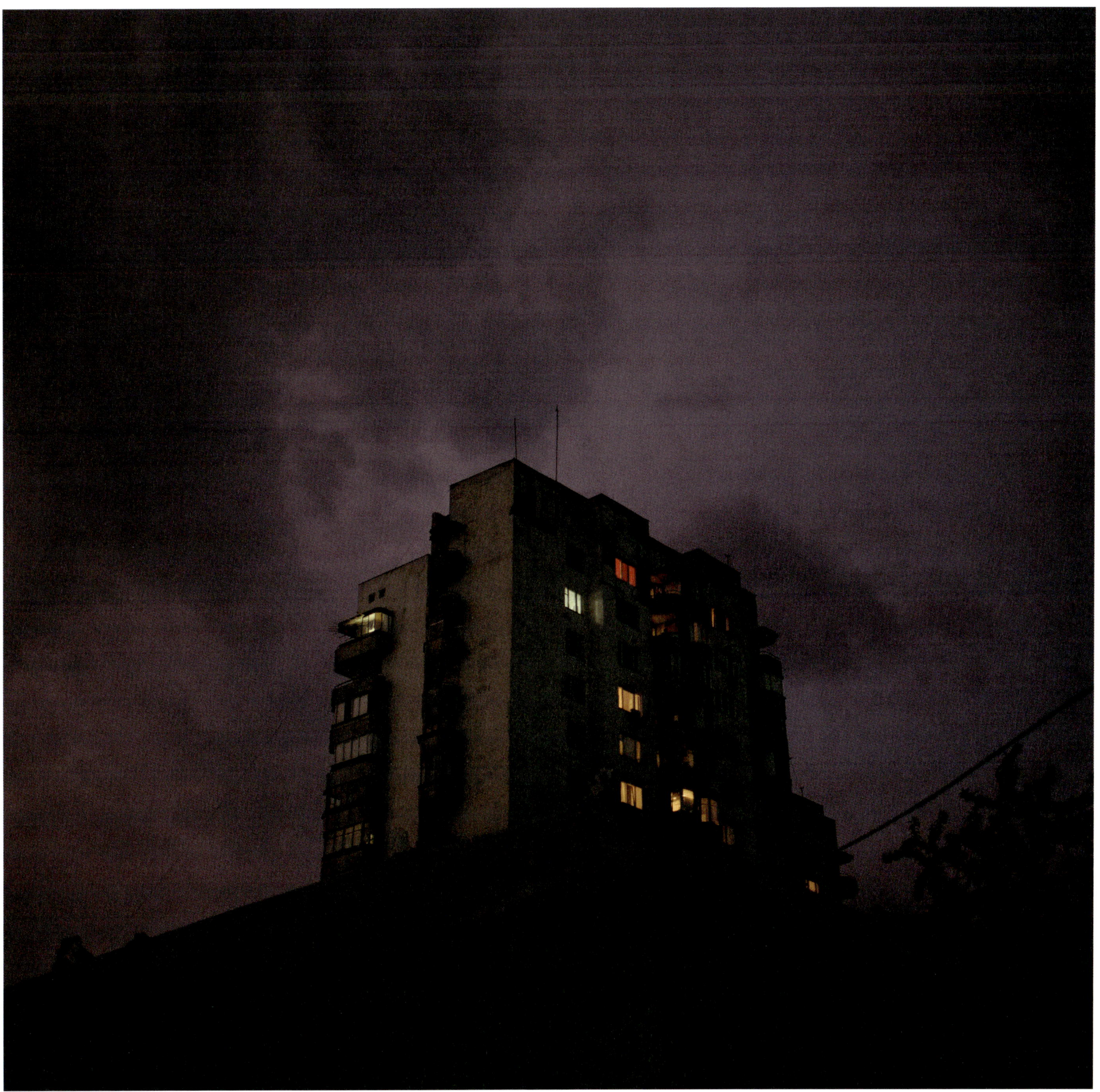

Tiraspol, Transnistria 2015

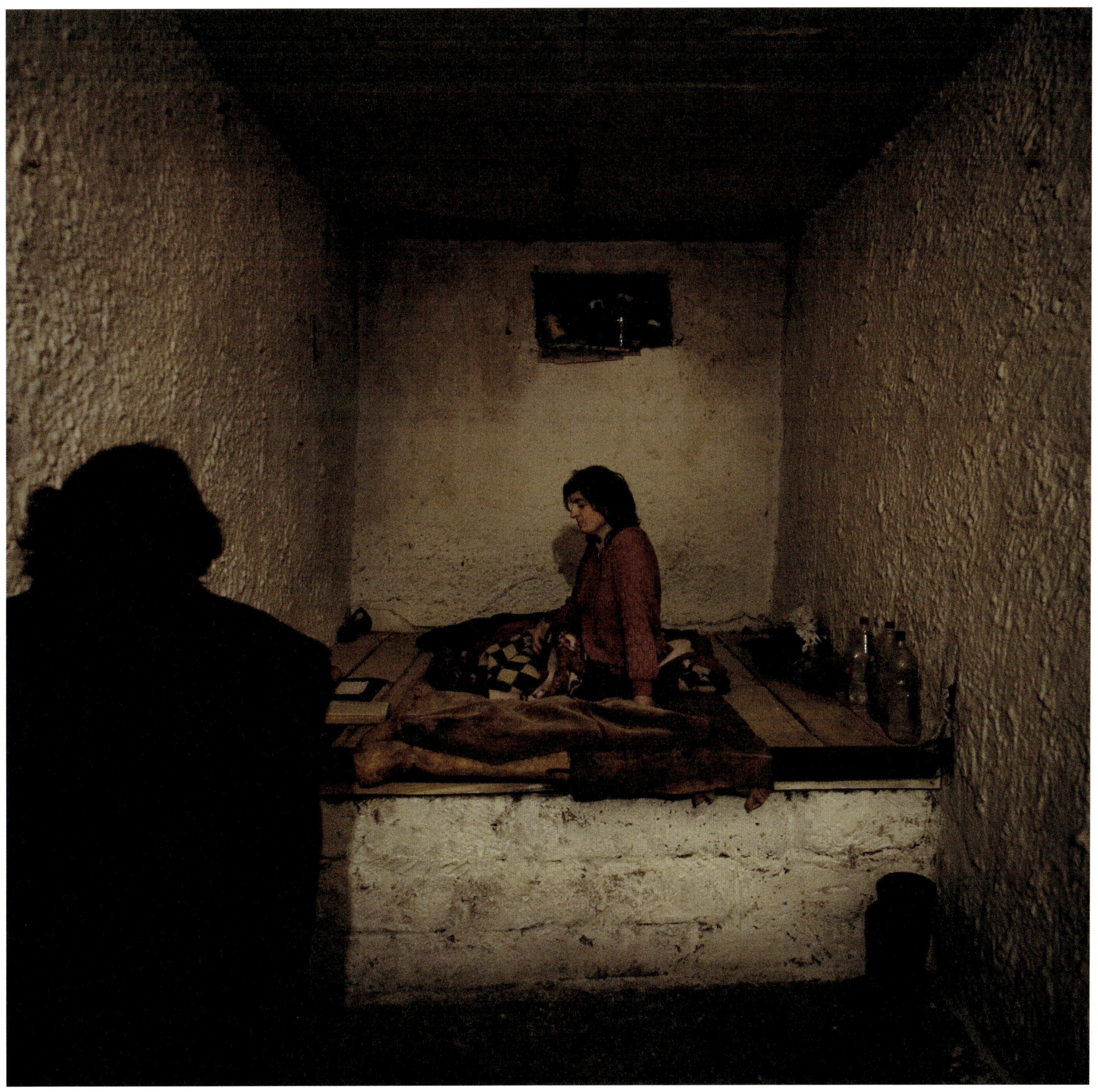

Holding cell, Hîncești 2006

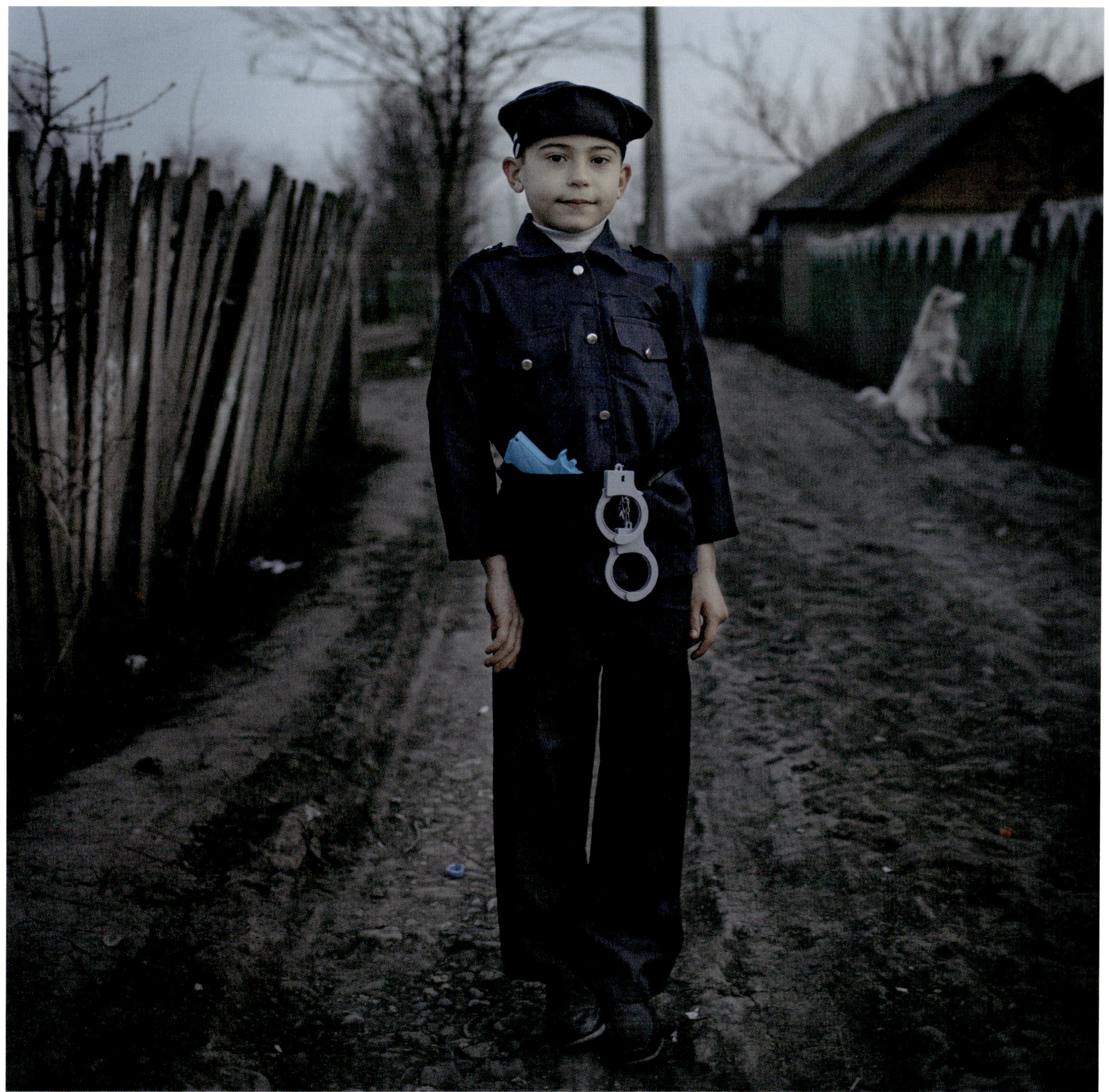

Hugh jr, Baroncea 2014

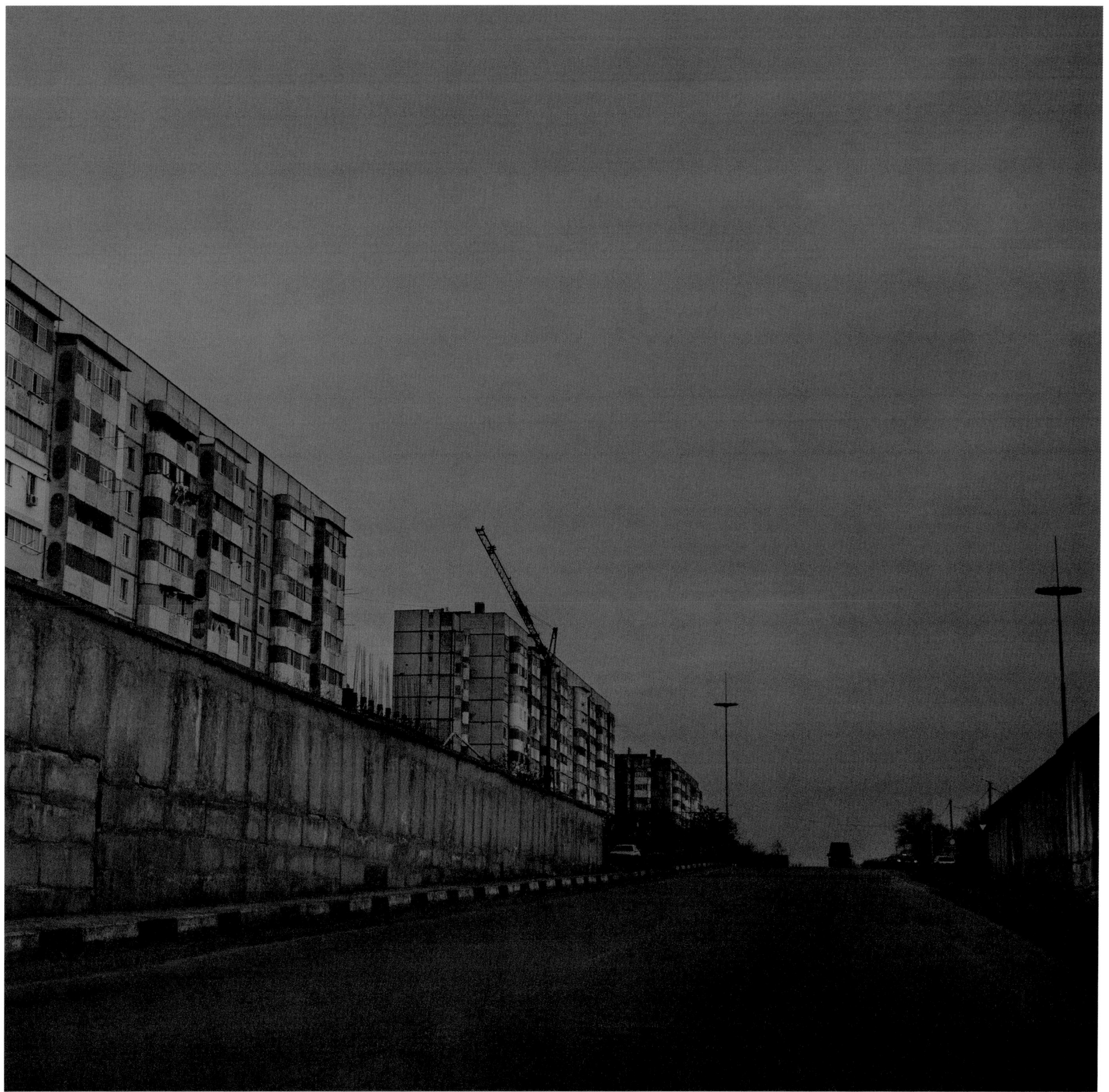

Bălţi 2014

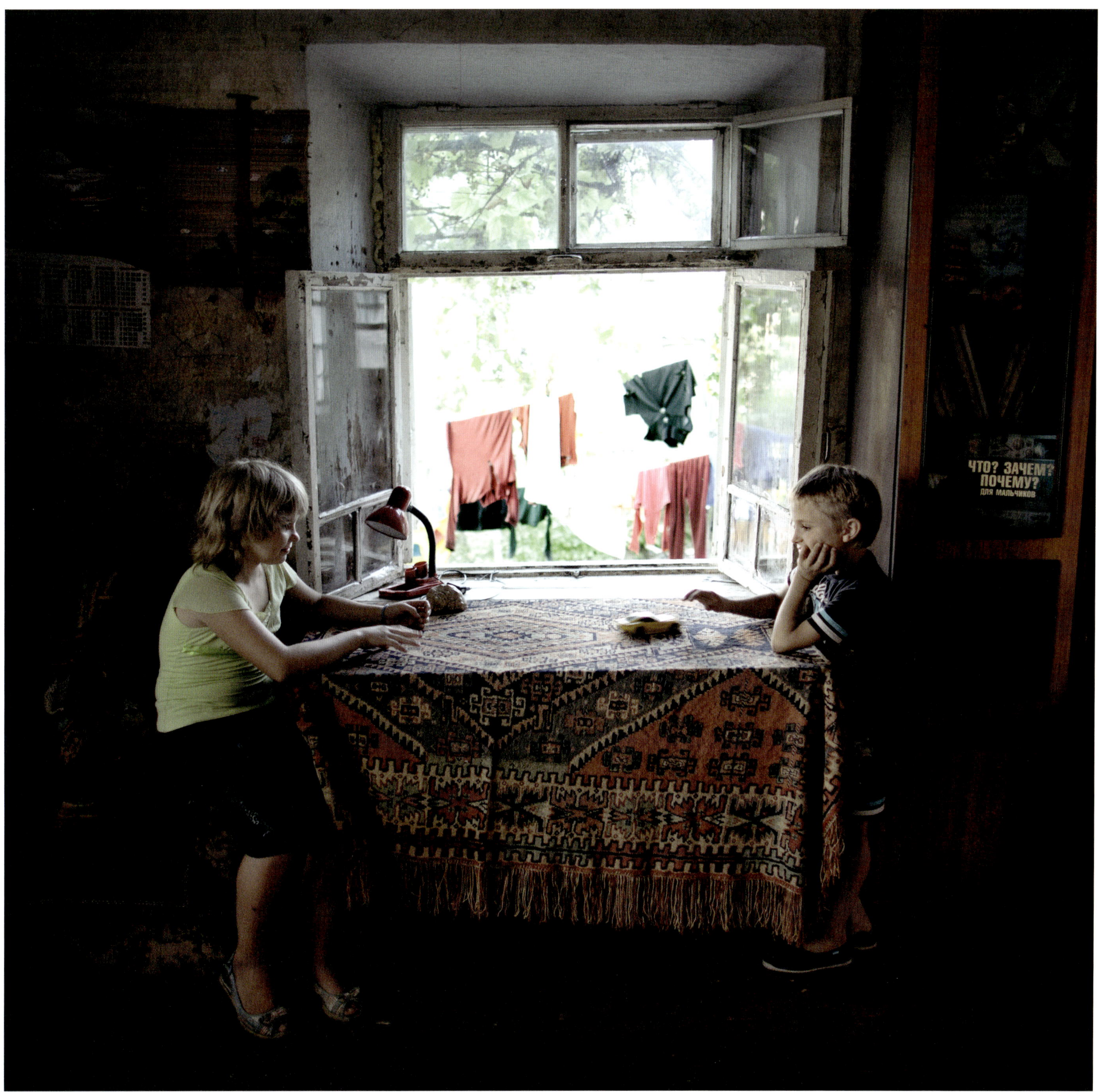

Codru 2015

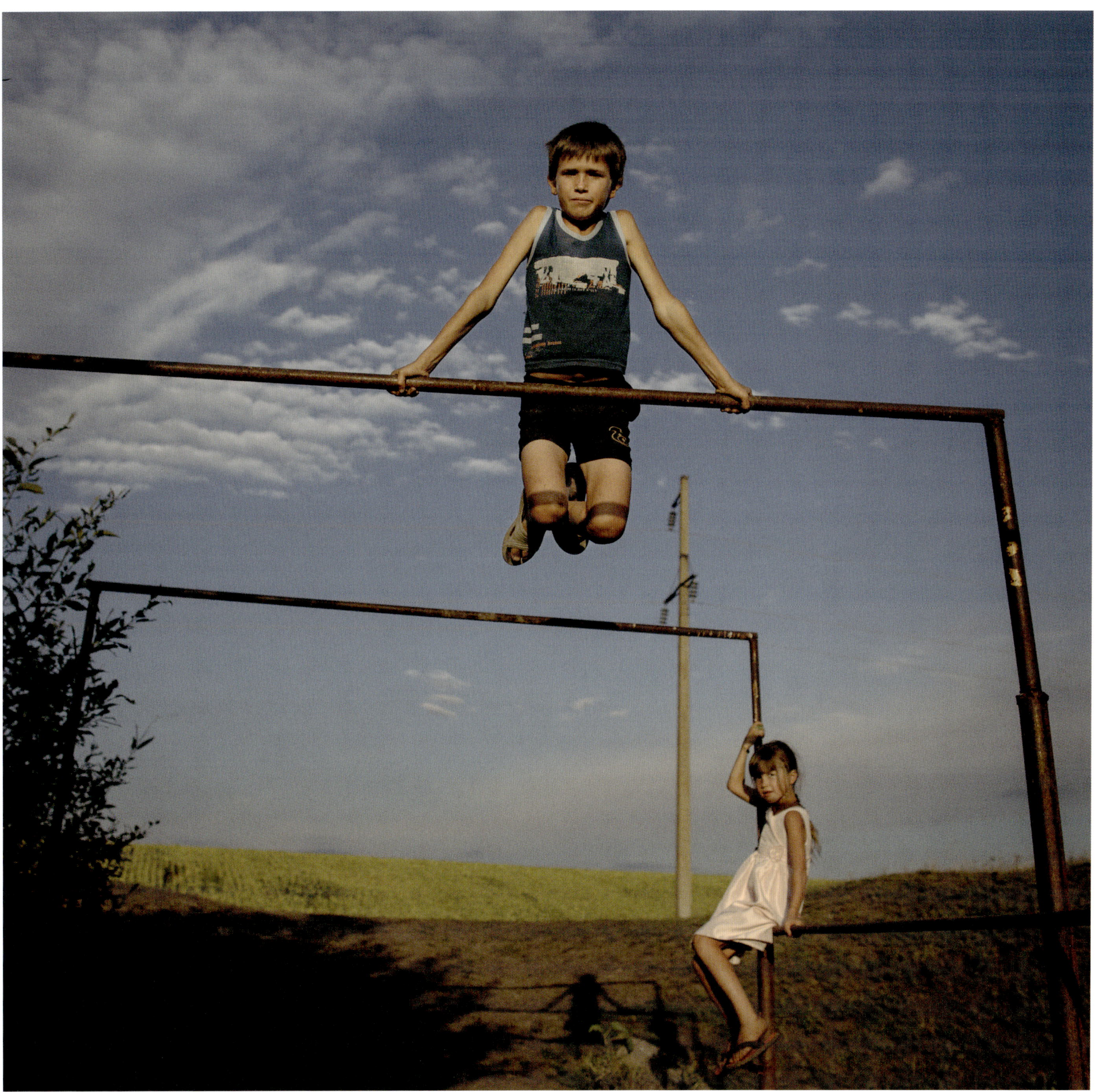

Beniamin and Kristina, Chetrosu 2016

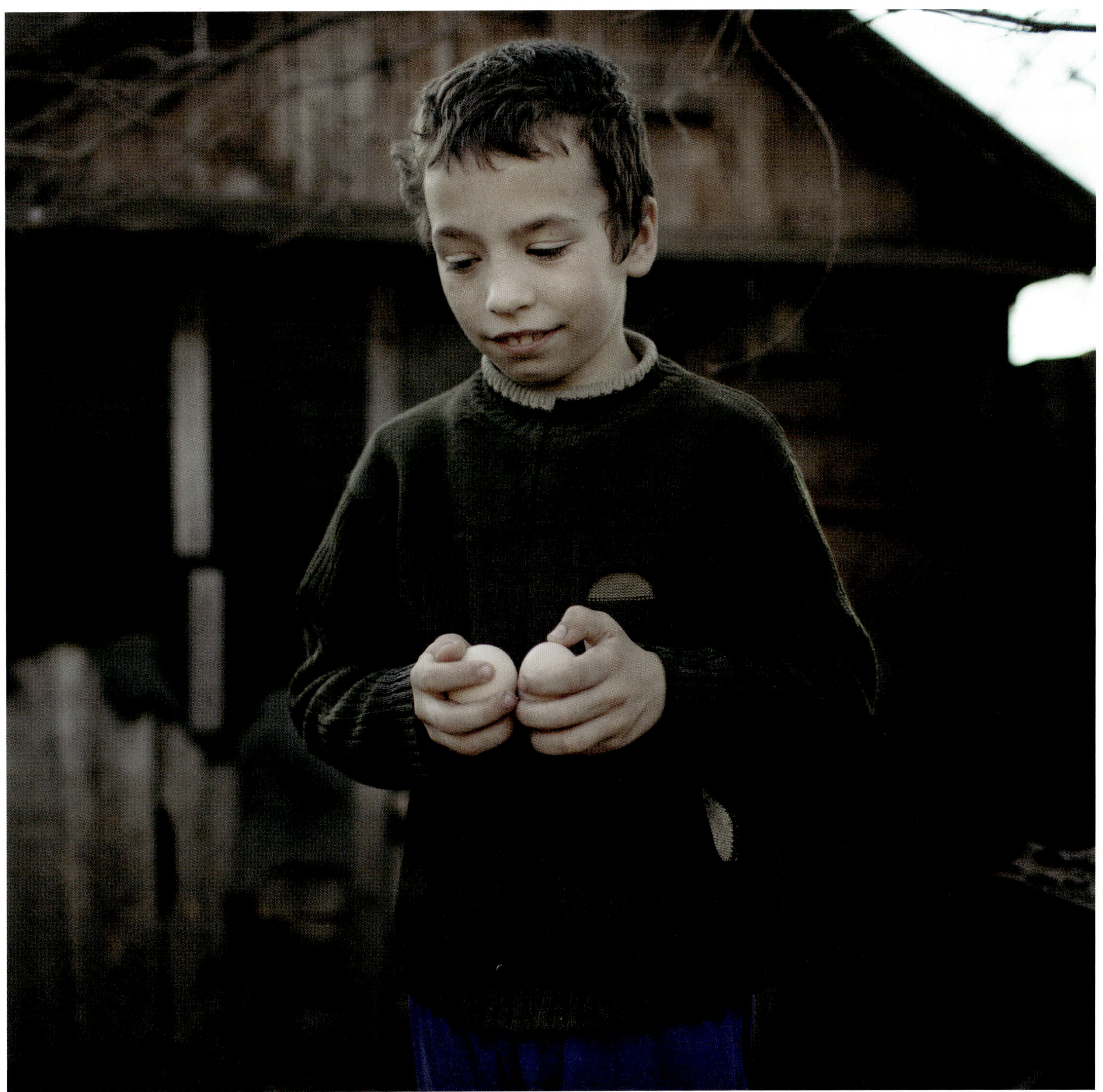

Artur, Baroncea 2014

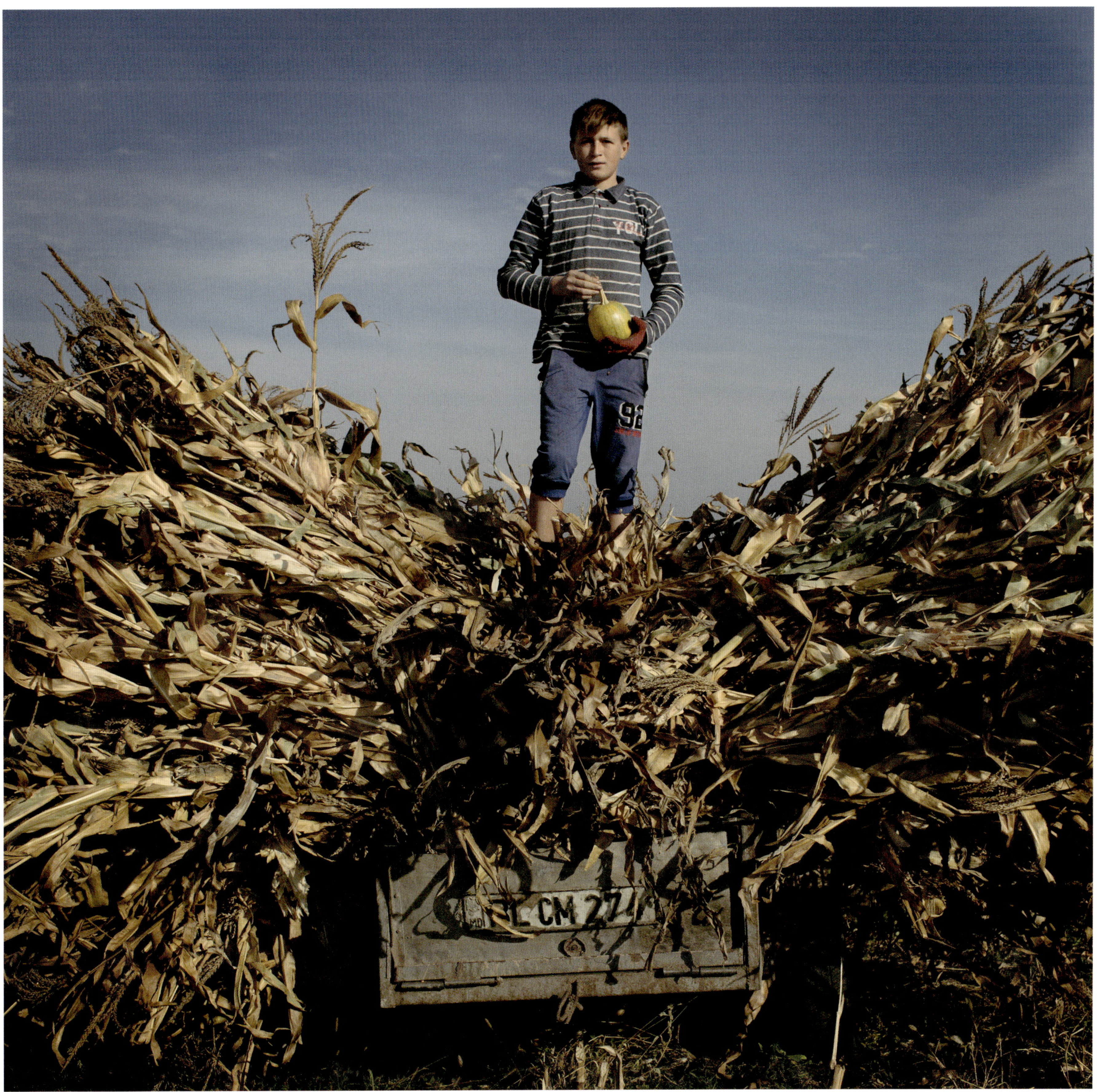

Iosif, Chetrosu 2016

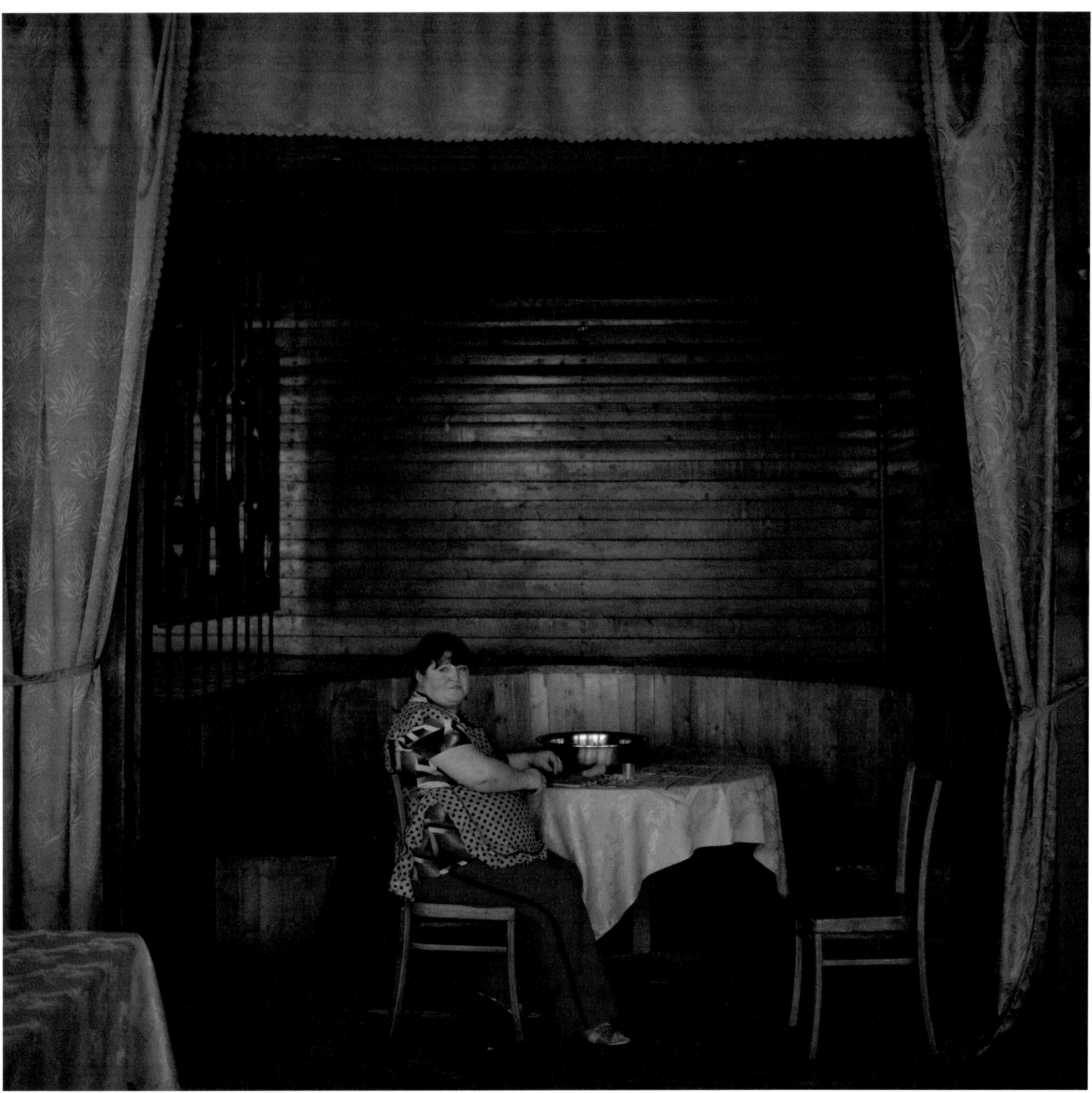

Road stop, Moldova 2015

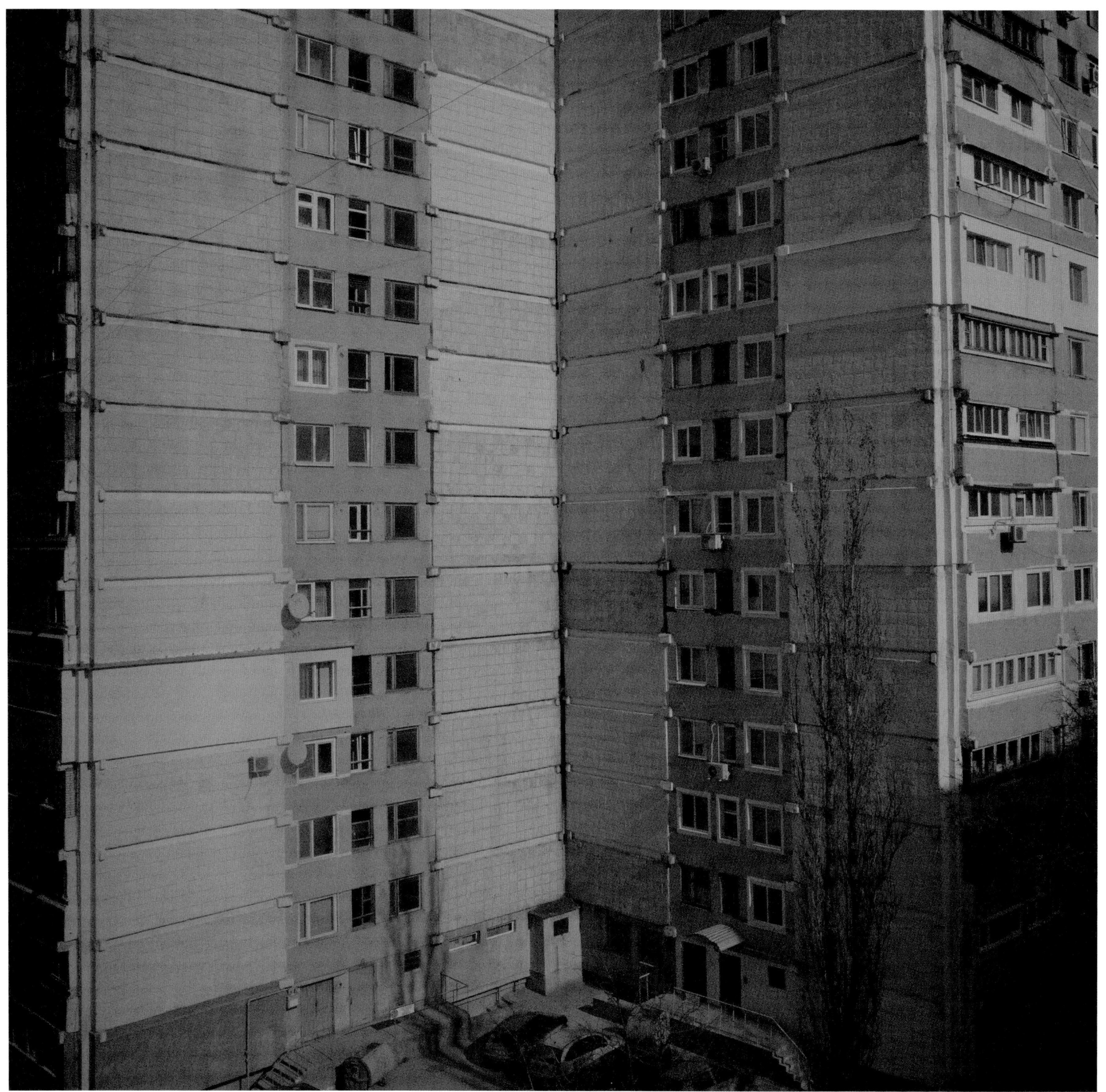

Chisinau 2006

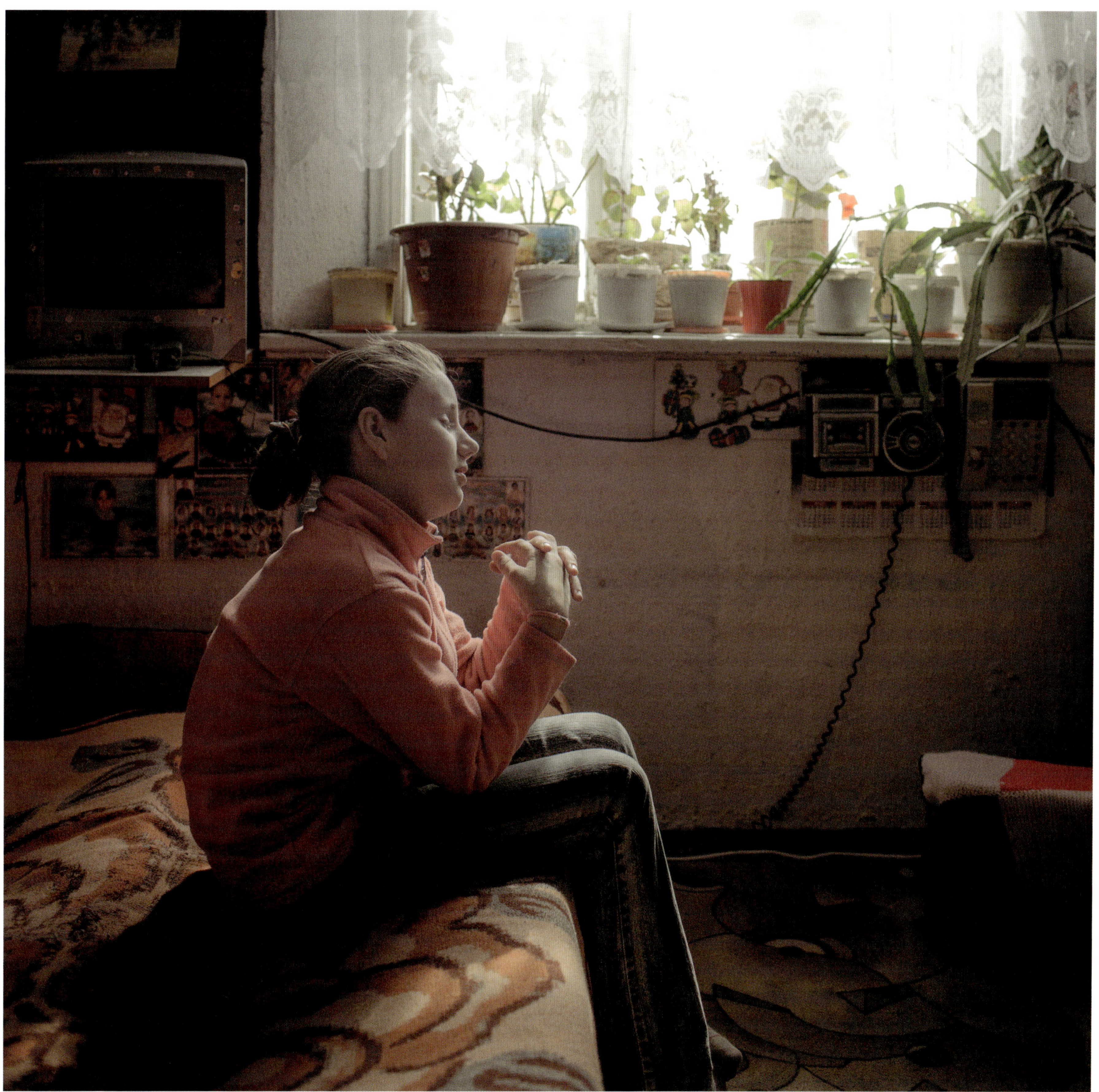

Ania, Baroncea 2014

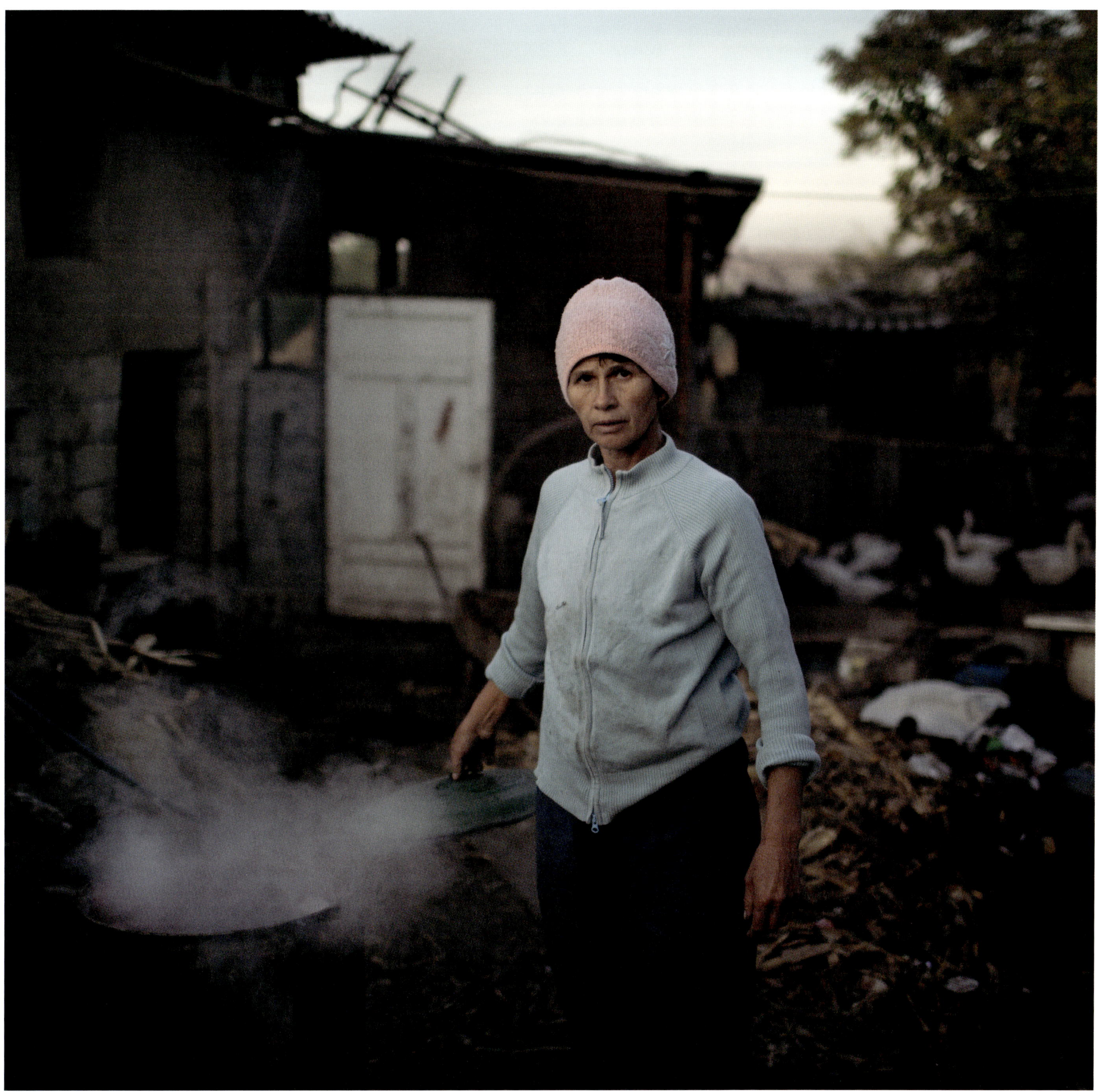

Zina, Chetrosu 2016

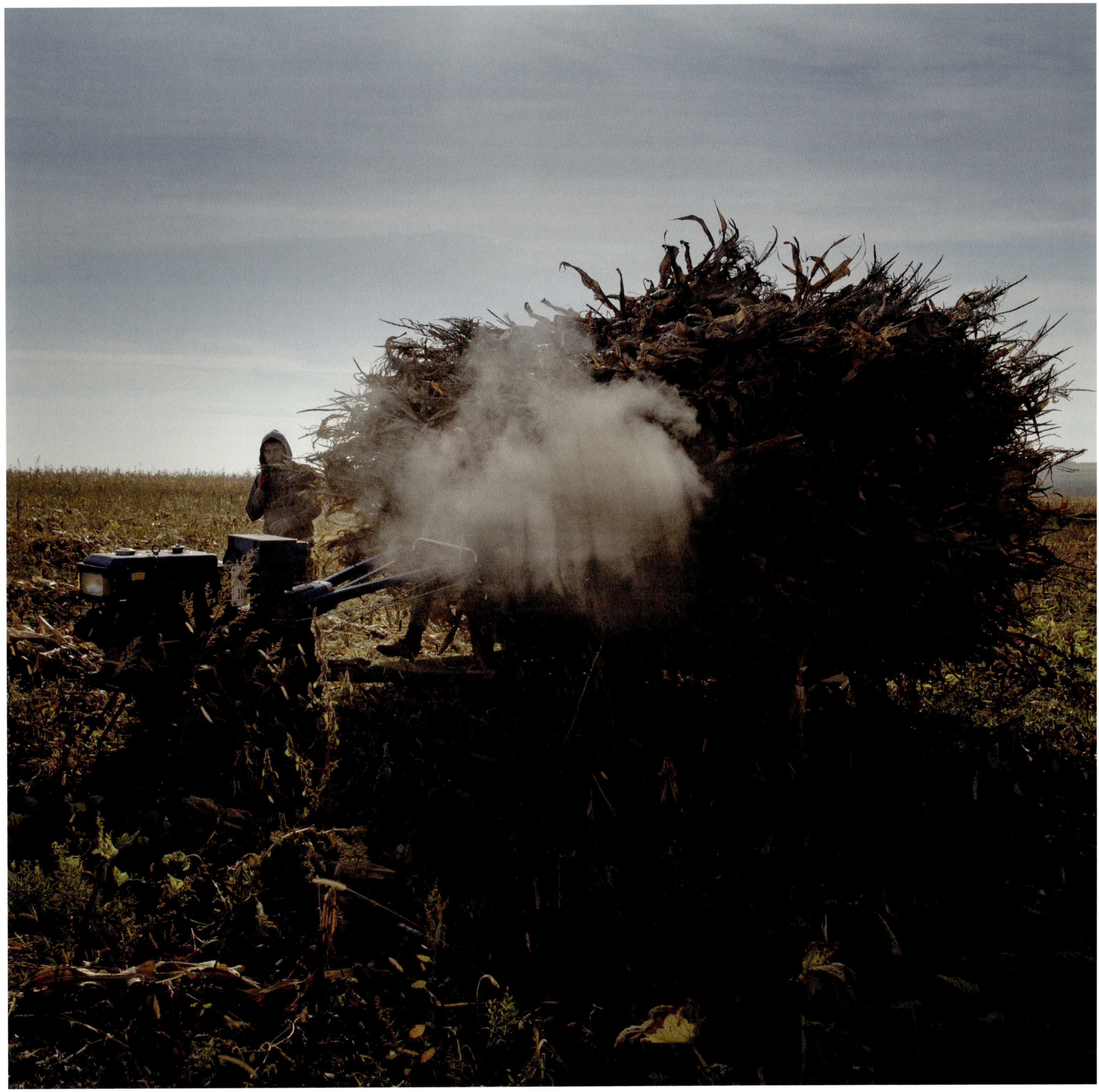

Chetrosu 2016

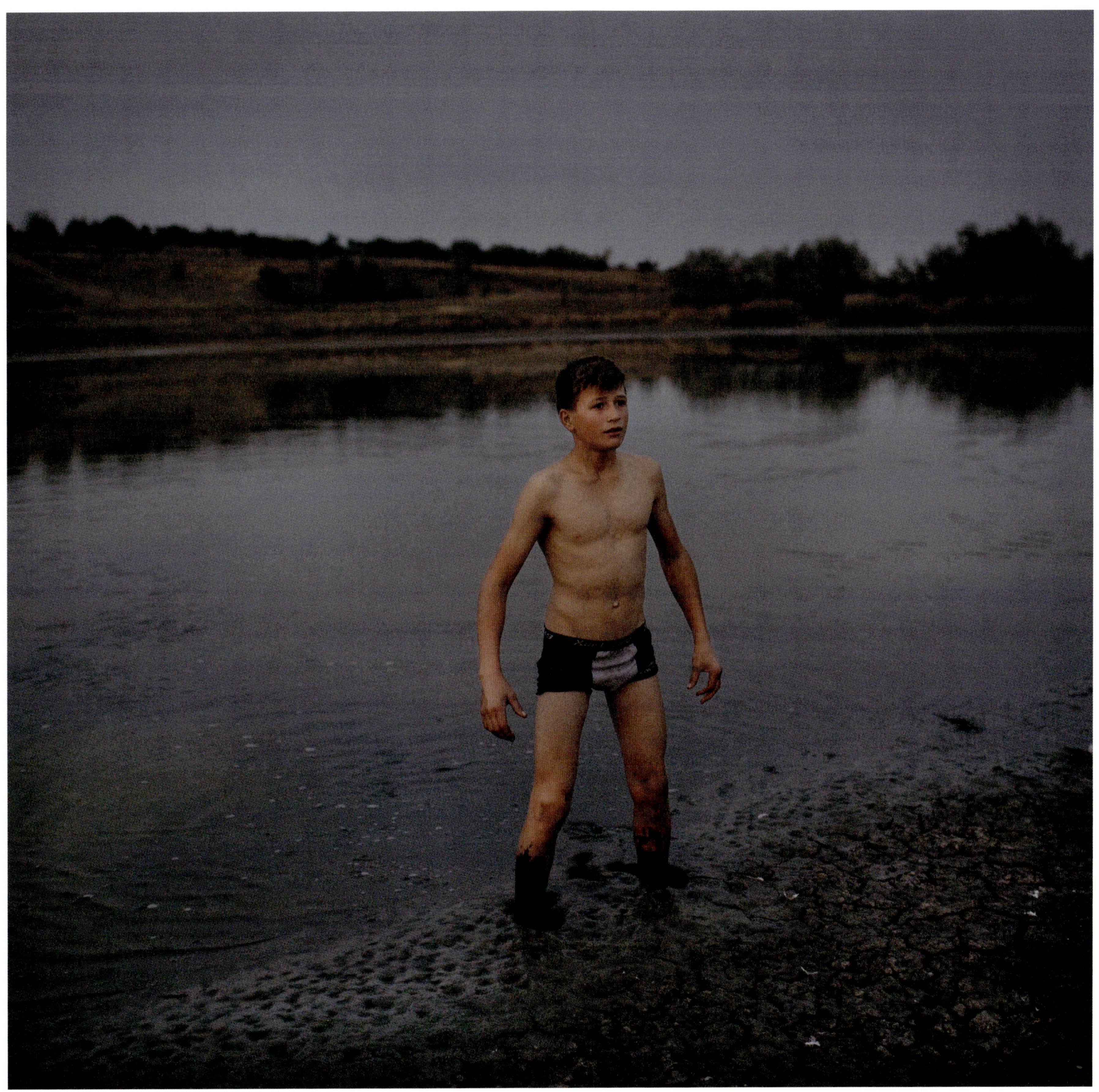

Iosif, Chetrosu 2016

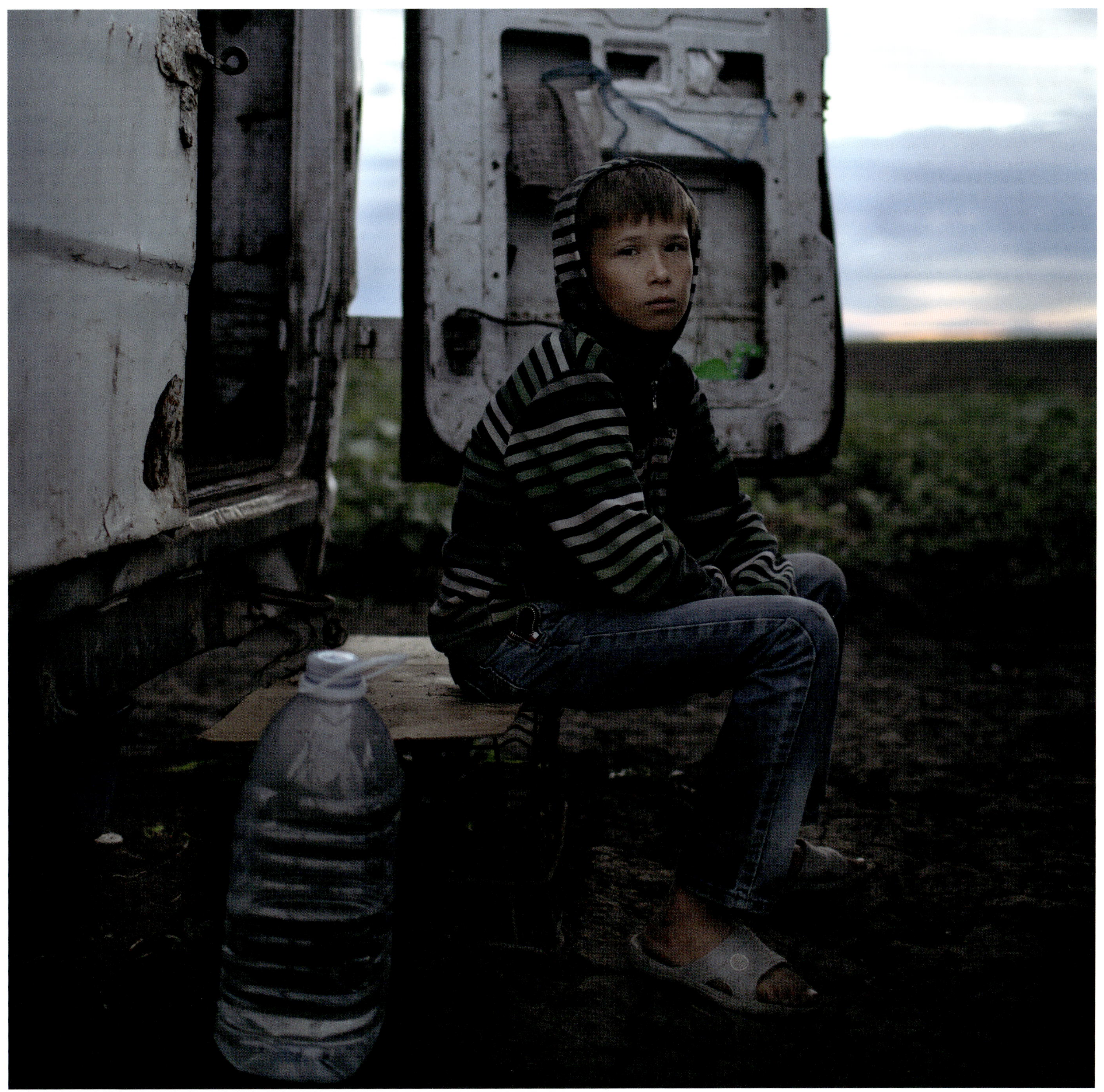

Beniamin, Chetrosu 2016

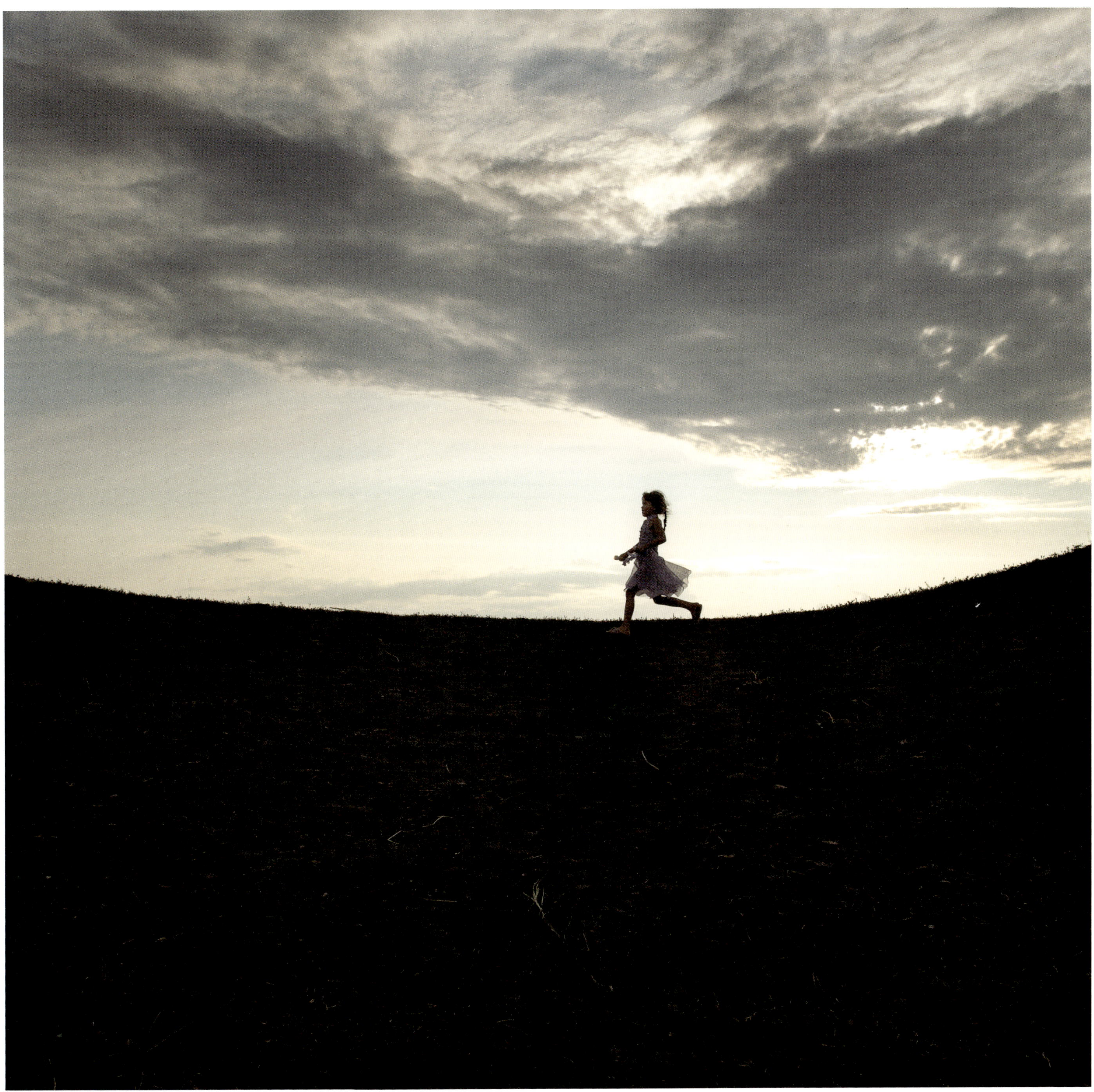

Kristina, Chetrosu 2015

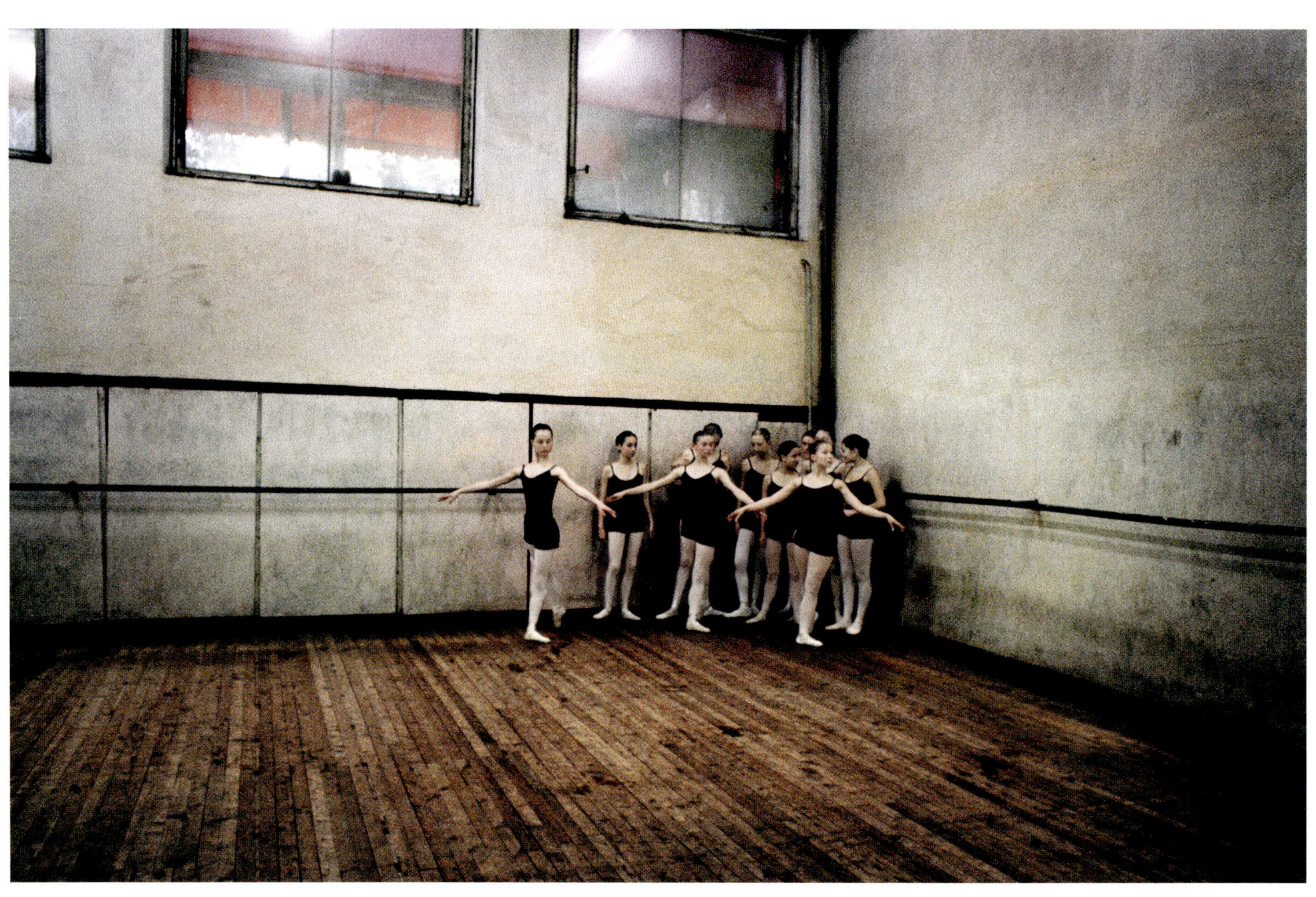

Moldova Ballet

I discovered the National Opera and Ballet Theatre of Moldova on my first visit to the country in June 2005. At the time, it had been days since I had taken a picture and it felt as though the trip wasn't going anywhere. All I really wanted was to go back home.

Walking past a beautiful, well-worn historical building in downtown Chisinau, I asked my interpreter whom was playing the piano inside, and why someone was yelling strict instructions? He told me it was a school for ballet dancers. My curiosity was piqued: it wasn't what I had expected to stumble across on that trip.

Inside, the 16-year-old dance students were going through their daily exercises. I learned the school is known for the fierce competition among its students. Many young girls and boys saw the ballet as a route to a better life and travel abroad. Twelve boys and twelve girls around eight years of age are accepted into gender-specific ballet classes every year. They stay for nine years, training a minimum of five hours a day in addition to their normal lessons. Each year, numbers in the classes diminish, as those not considered talented enough are weeded out of the programme.

Throughout the following decade that I spent photographing Moldova, I often thought back to the ballet school I stumbled upon that difficult day in Chisinau. The grace and determination I saw in the dancers captivated me. When I had nearly lost my own will to continue, I had been inspired – not only as a photographer, but also as a person exploring the unknown. I learned to understand myself better, to grow and see the unexpected, instead of losing faith in my projects.

The photographs of the ballet school in Moldova still bring me back to my earliest years exploring the country and remind me of my development as a photographer. I also feel they are emblematic of the hopes and dreams I witnessed in one of Europe's "forgotten" countries, which I have come to think of as the Silent Land.

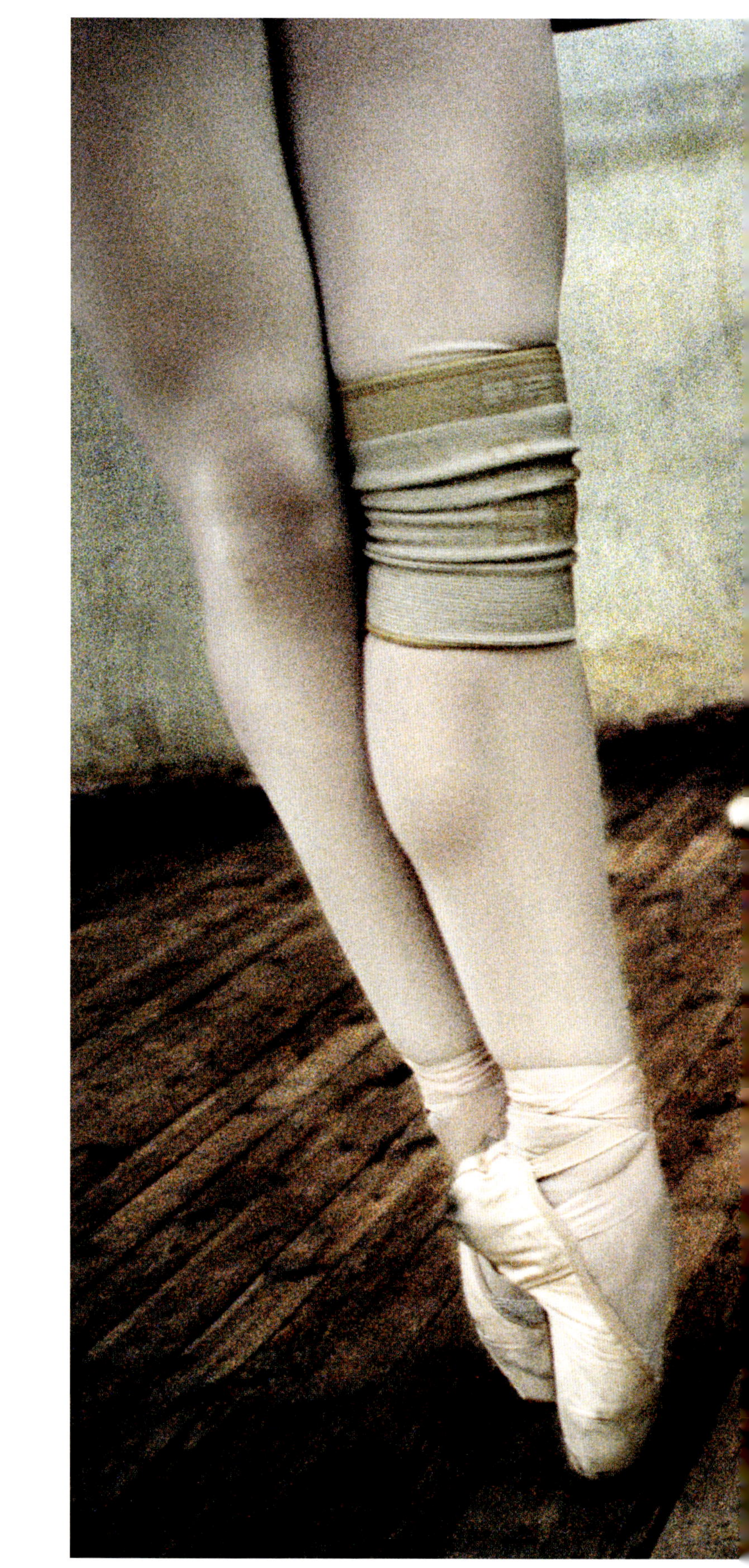

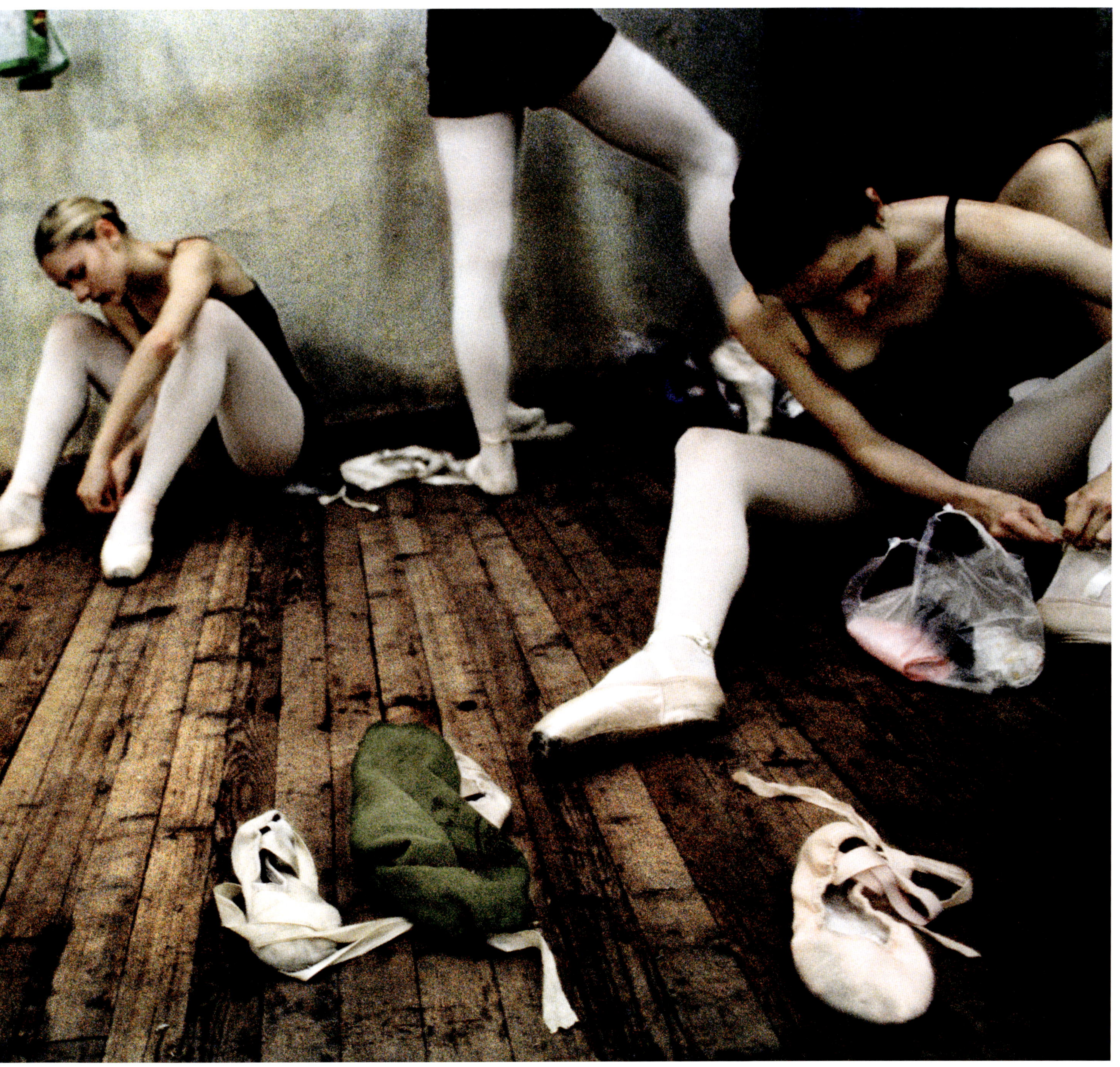

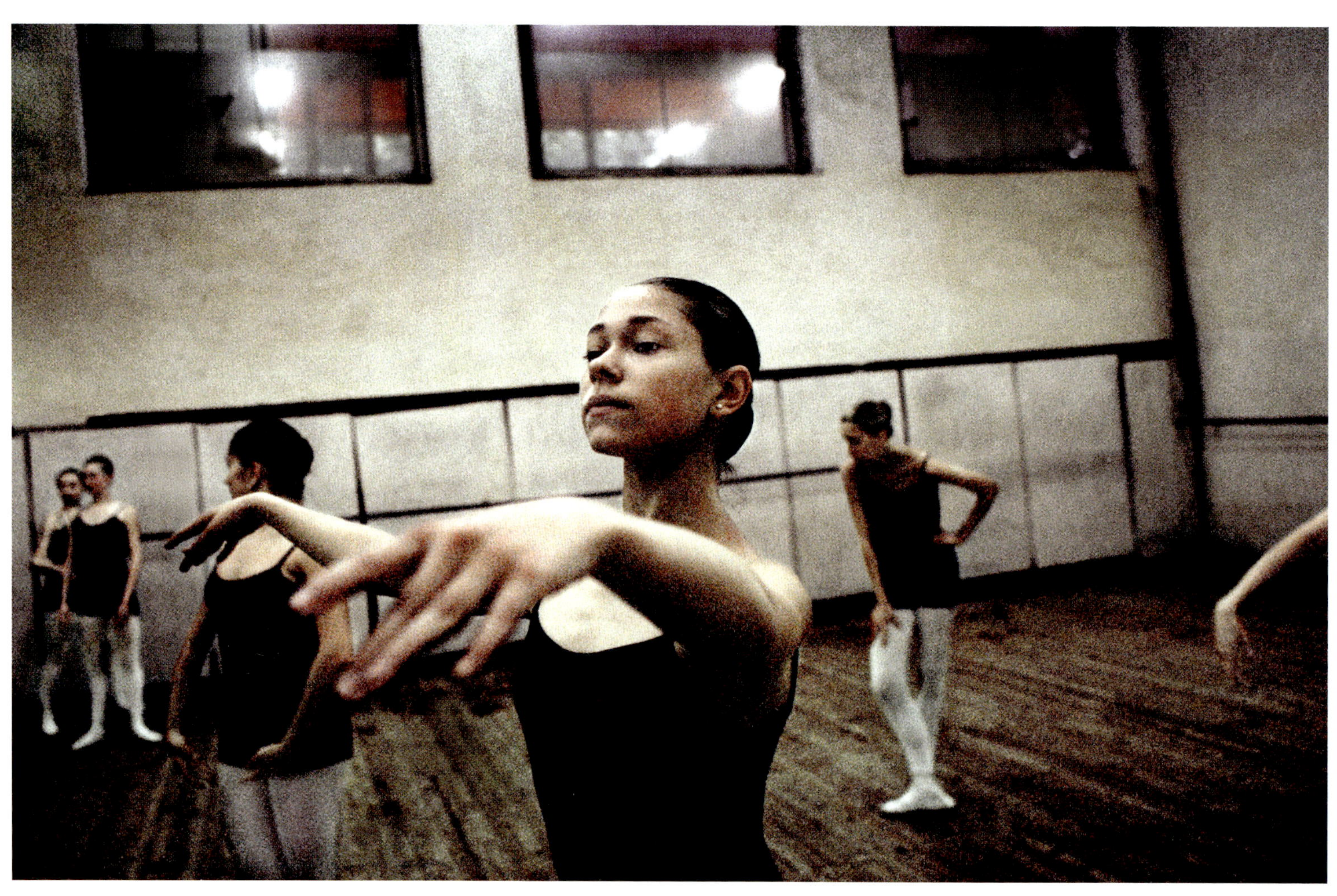

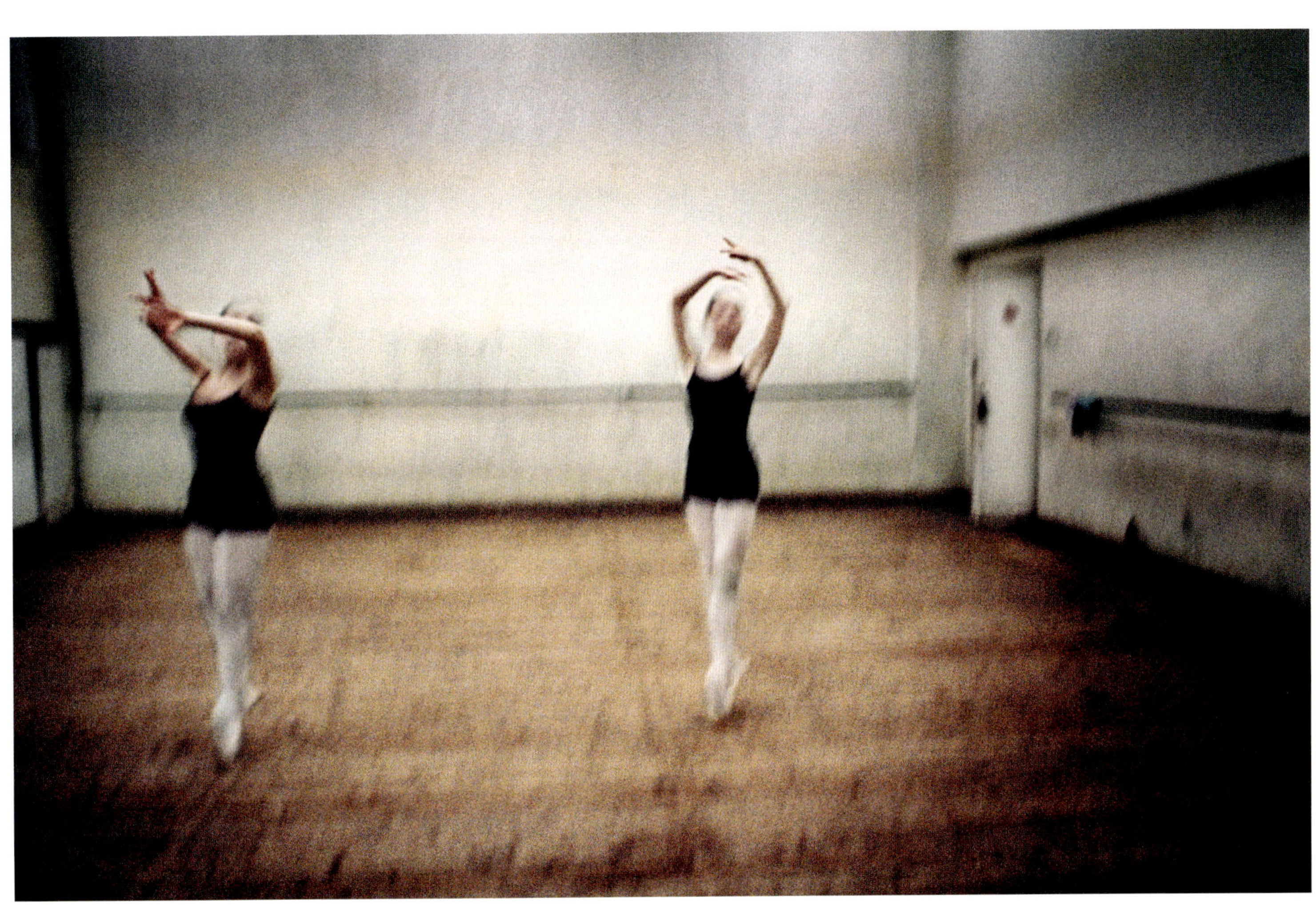

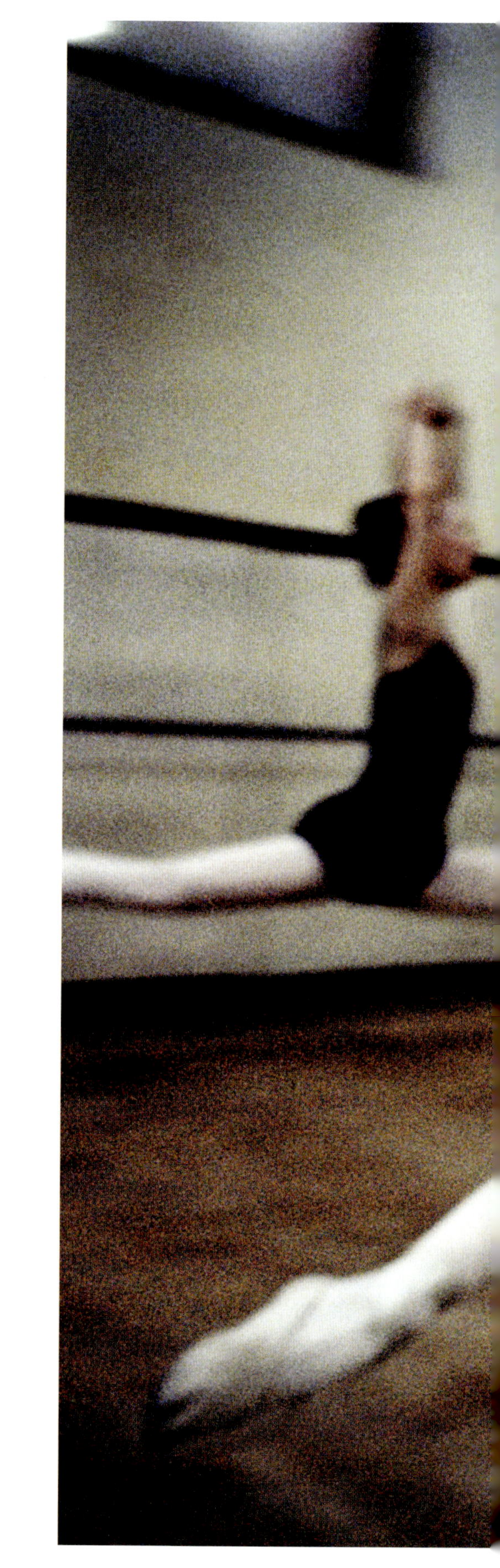

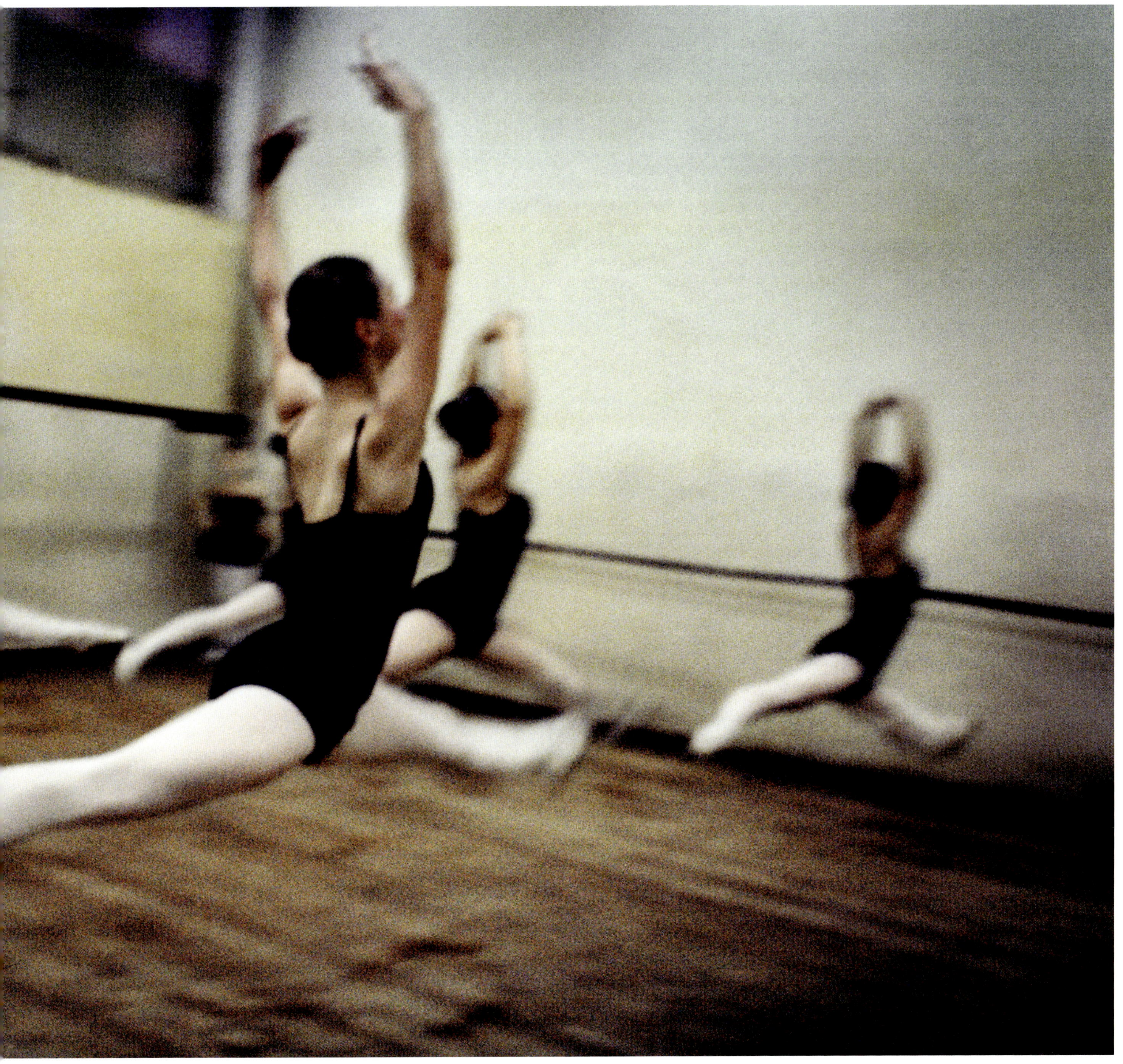

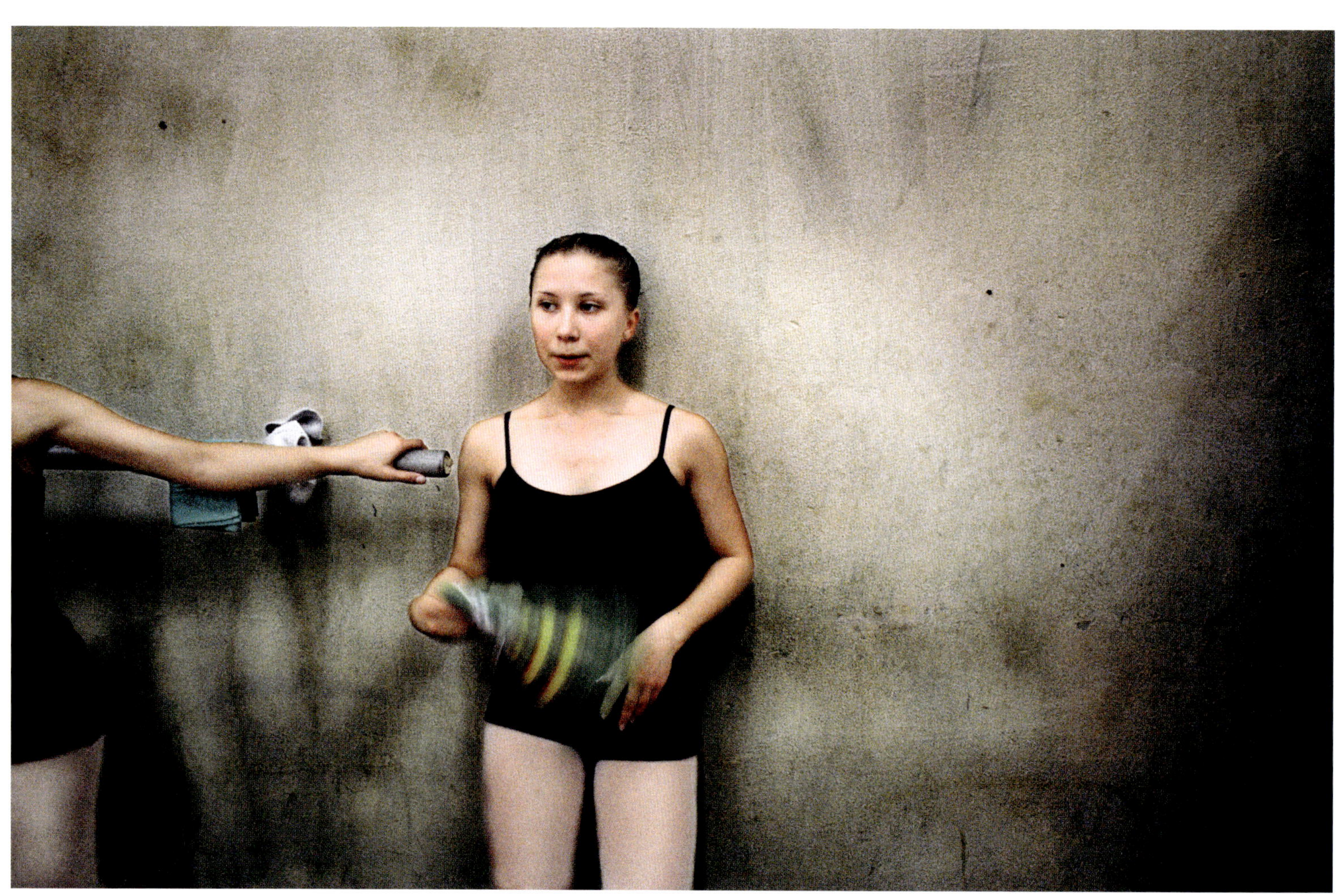

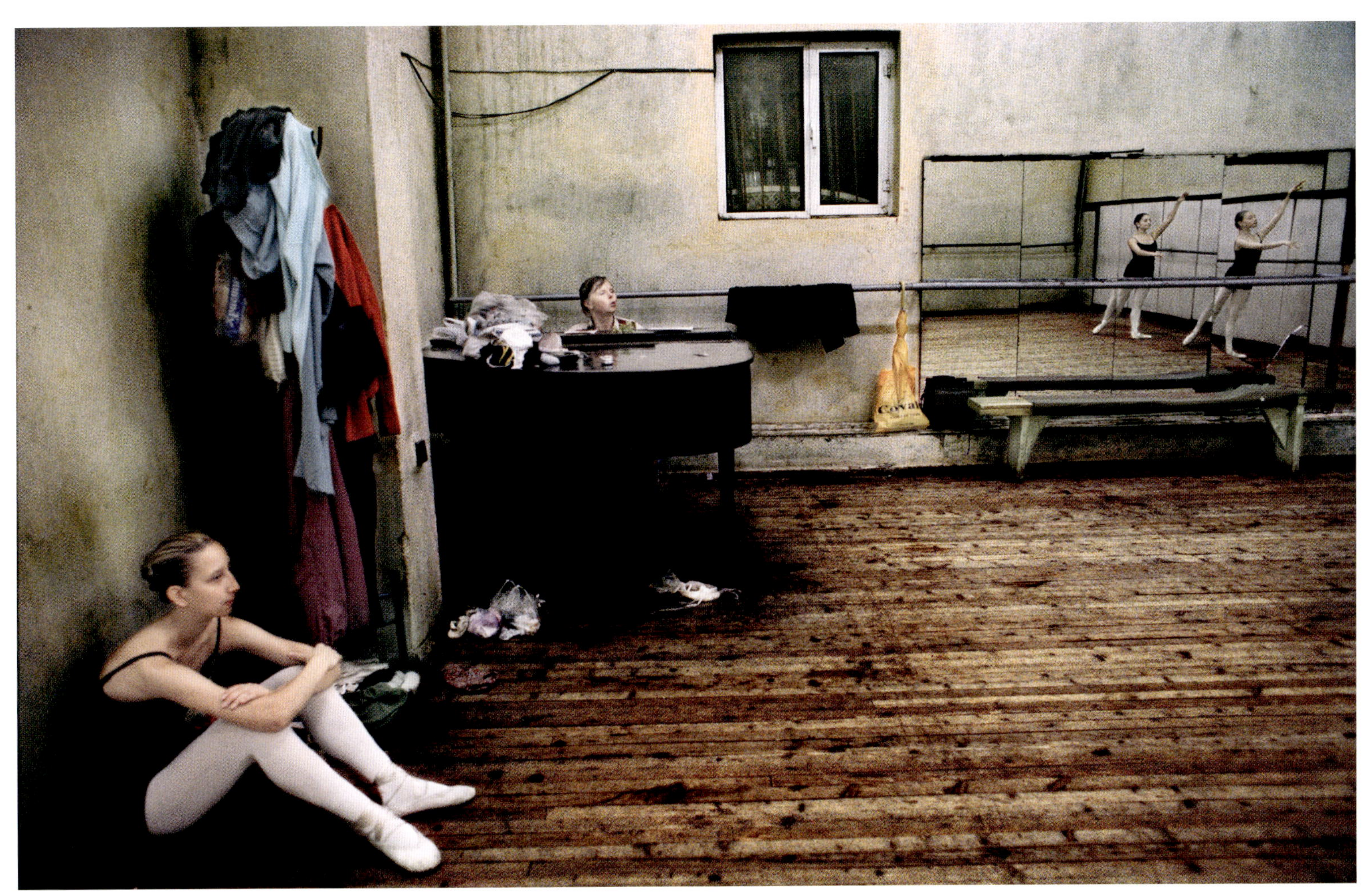

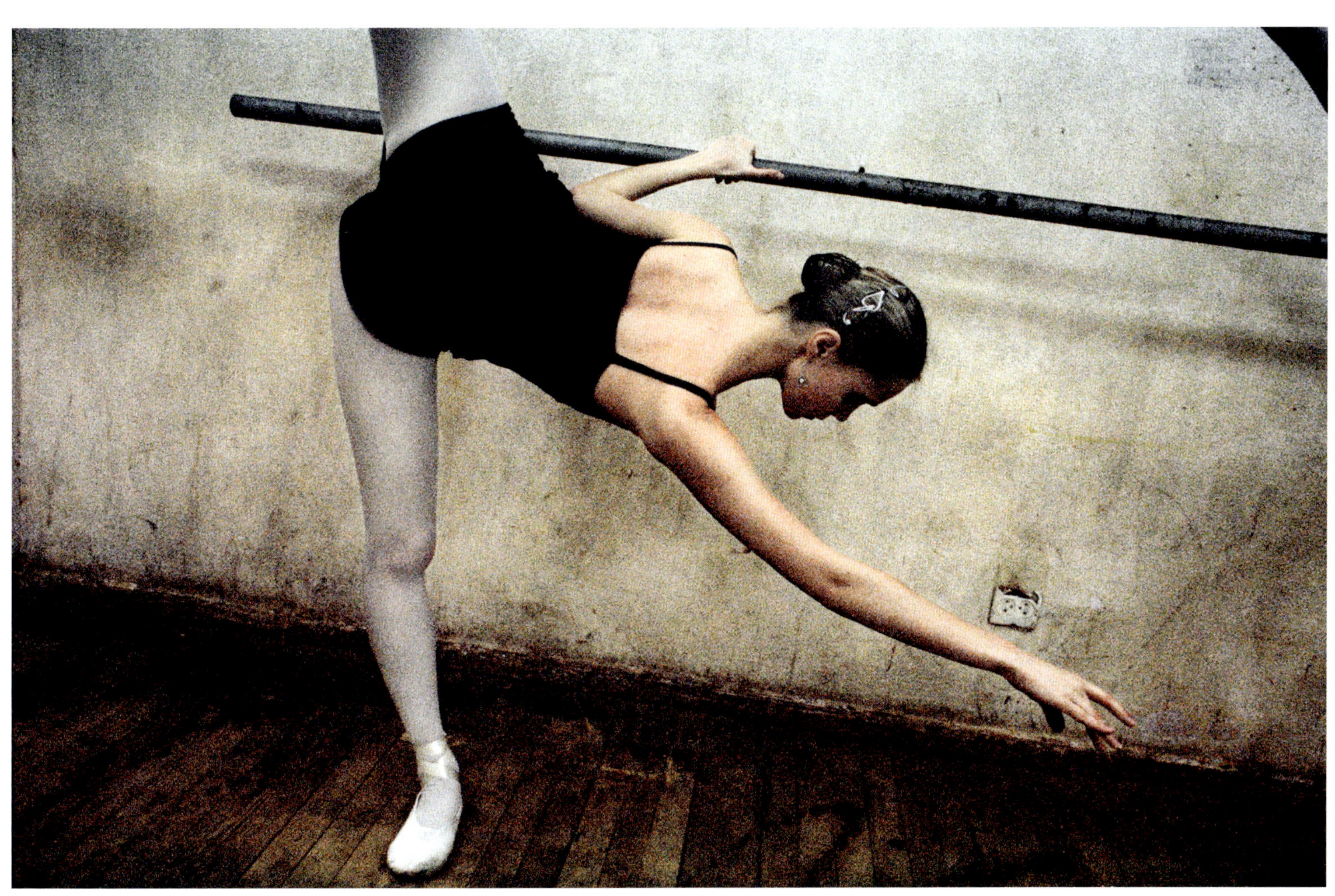

Silent Land

I see myself in those I photograph and I often wonder what it would be like if their lives had been mine. The connection feels personal, as if we share a story, but one that is not my own.

When I first travelled to Moldova in 2005, I grew close to the people and the country in the context of suffering and social problems. These were the stories that drew me there and coloured my perceptions.

Three month-long trips later, I had images of prisoners, victims of human trafficking and domestic violence, but my larger picture of Moldova felt incomplete. I wanted to understand more and to do so I felt I needed to get away from my usual reporting style; to leave my comfort zone and instead try to understand everyday life in Moldova.

Moldova is wedged between Ukraine and Romania and is little known outside its own borders. There I met people with integrity, a striking seriousness that captured my imagination from the moment I arrived. I saw the people, their poverty and their dignity. I saw a beauty in the brutal and fragile reality I experienced.

It is often hard to get people to see the point of allowing a photographer to come into their lives to take pictures. And as a photographer, it is not easy to portray a day where nothing unusual happens. Capturing this daily life with intimacy and proximity is challenging and doing it well takes time.

When I began photographing in Moldova, it was an isolated society that had recently voted for the return of communism. I arrived in villages with light-blue-coloured houses decorated with beautiful wooden carvings, where children played with whatever they could find, often looked after by older women, known as babushkas. But below the picturesque surface, there was an identity crisis – a fight between old and new, between the Russian- and Romanian-speakers, between East and West.

Eight years later, the communists were voted out of power once more. The borders had opened, and I arrived in a country that had become emptier and quieter. More than one million people had left, almost a quarter of the population.

My project gained new urgency. I returned to places where I had photographed before and searched for the same people. I tried to go beyond the reports in the mainstream media and document the lives of those who never would have made it into the news. I found that the local stories lost behind the headlines were the most nuanced way to understand the profound changes the country was going through.

Moldova possesses a beauty that contrasts starkly with the hard lives of most Moldovans. Rolling countryside and dark soil once made this country rich. Prior to the fall of the Soviet Union, Russians bought summerhouses here, drank local wine and beer, and enjoyed summer's fresh fruit and vegetables. It was considered stylish to speak Russian and villagers worked in collectives. Today only memories remain from that era, but many say that it was better in the past –everyone was equal back then. There were jobs and there was food on the table.

"Nowadays, everyone thinks for themselves and all that matters is showing others how well you're doing," says Ion, father of the Gradinari family in Chetrosu.

To be the most beautiful girl at the annual school ball your family will have to live on virtually nothing for two months just to buy or hire a nice dress for a single evening, say the twin sisters Mihaela and Karina Dumitraschuk, who caused a stir in their village by refusing to go to the school ball precisely for this reason.

Today the sisters study marketing at a state-run boarding school in Chisinau, the capital, with other students from the countryside.

Moldova has changed fundamentally since 2005, as have I and many of those I have met. I can't always explain why a story catches my imagination; the pictures have to speak for themselves. Every time I head back, I think about what drives me to do this. But I have learned that once something has got under my skin, it can be difficult to let go. I want to know more, to understand the country and get to know the people.

I see myself in those I photograph and I often wonder what it would be like if their lives had been mine. The connection feels personal, as if we share a story, but one that is not my own.

I would like to give a special thank you to everyone who has contributed to this book, especially to the Gradinaris and Mihaela and Karina Dumitraschuk for your openness and hospitality.

Thank you also to Rufus and Betty, Daniel Nilsson, Elin Berge, Sara and Sebastian Sjöström, Roza Baban, Linda Stark, Anna Claesson, Anna Clarén, Karen Söderberg, Sveta Malteva, Patric Leo, Jeppe Wikström, Jan Broman, Marc Prust, Jonathan Saruk and everyone else who in some way has been involved in this project and helped to bring this book to fruition.

Silent Land has been made possible with support from Anna Lindhs Utvecklingsstipendium, World Press Photo, Saint-Brieuc Photoreporter Grant, the Swedish Arts Grants Committee and Längmanska Kulturfonden.

© Bokförlaget Max Ström, 2017
Photography and text Åsa Sjöström
Design Patric Leo
Translation Nick Chipperfield
Repro Linjepunkt, Falun
Print Livonia Print, Latvia, 2017

ISBN 978-91-7126-420-6
www.maxstrom.se